Facilitating for Learning

Facilitating for Learning

Tools for Teacher Groups of All Kinds

David Allen
Tina Blythe

Foreword by
Ron Ritchhart

TEACHERS COLLEGE PRESS
TEACHERS COLLEGE | COLUMBIA UNIVERSITY
NEW YORK AND LONDON

Published by Teachers College Press, 1234 Amsterdam Avenue, New York, NY 10027

The authors would like to acknowledge the following works were used by permission: Figure 4.2: Harvard Project Zero, 1992; Figure 5.2: the School Reform Initiative; Figure 6.2: Jossey-Bass; Figure 10.1: Wiley.

Library of Congress Cataloging-in-Publication Data

Allen, David, 1961–
    Facilitating for learning : tools for teacher groups of all kinds / David Allen, Tina Blythe ; foreword by Ron Ritchhart.
        pages cm
    Includes bibliographical references and index.
    ISBN 978-0-8077-5738-3 (pbk. : alk. paper) — ISBN 978-0-8077-7438-0 (ebook)
    1. Group work in education. 2. Professional learning communities. I. Blythe, Tina, 1964– II. Title.
    LB1032.A43 2015
    371.39'5–dc23   2015013563

ISBN 978-0-8077-5738-3 (paper)
ISBN 978-0-8077-7438-0 (ebook)

Printed on acid-free paper
Manufactured in the United States of America

22 21 20 19 18 17 16 15   8 7 6 5 4 3 2 1

Contents

PART III: OPPORTUNITIES AND CHALLENGES

The "Wants" of Professional Learning

"For classrooms to be cultures of thinking for students, schools must be cultures of thinking for teachers." So says principle number six from the Worldwide Cultures of Thinking Project, which I have directed for the past decade. It appears last on the list not because it is of less importance than those that precede it, but because it grounds all the other principles and, without this key tenet, the others—such as "Skills are insufficient; we must also have the disposition to use them," "To understand both how and what our students are learning we must strive to make their thinking visible," or "The development of thinking and understanding is largely a social endeavor"—are unlikely to take hold beyond the superficial implementation of a few useful techniques and practices.

Developing a community in which deep and rich discussions about teaching, learning, and thinking are a fundamental part of teachers' ongoing experience provides the foundation for nurturing students' thinking and learning. And yet, the full realization of this principle is elusive in far too many schools. What does it take to go beyond a series of teacher PD sessions—sessions that some label as *professional development*, while others refer to them as *professional distraction*, or worse, *professional discouragement* sessions—to be more about adults learning in collaborative inquiry with one another? In part, it means we must do some radical rethinking of schooling as usual, calling into question some common practices and timeworn assumptions.

Chief among the practices that need to be rethought is the tendency to view professional learning merely as time to hear about the latest instructional innovation or top-down mandate in a cursory fashion—the topic *du jour*, as it were. Such a view encourages a coverage mentality that focuses on "learning about" rather than an in-depth exploration. We know that isolated time spent on a topic isn't rich learning for students, and it isn't rich learning for teachers, either. Nor should we consider it professional learning when teachers come together for the purpose of completing work tasks, designing implementation plans, or planning units. Such tasks are important, but they aren't focused on learning how to be better teachers or helping us to be students of our students' learning. Instead, our precious time together needs to be clearly centered on going deeply into ideas and practices, reflecting on our ongoing efforts to apply ideas, raising questions and issues to which we truly want to be a party in finding the answers, and better understanding our students as learners and thinkers.

Many schools have already embarked on such rethinking around professional learning, or they are eager to do so. Often, a first step is the formation of professional learning communities or action-inquiry groups for this purpose. If such groups are to be successful, we must reject top-down, micromanaged, and heavily scripted PD and refocus our attention back where it belongs: on facilitating the learning of all group members. This kind of facilitation takes a specific set of skills, many of which can be gained from reading this book, putting the ideas into practice, and then critically reflecting on that practice. In addition, drawing on my own work in creating cultures of thinking, I have identified eight "wants" that seem to be helpful in fostering rich professional learning groups that both facilitators and school leaders might find useful as they seek to advance teachers' collaborative learning.

Adequate Time. There is never enough time for everything that needs to be done in schools. Therefore, our allocation of this scarce resource reflects our values as an organization. Most schools set aside scant time for professional learning, and yet we know that to truly understand anything complex and to build a community of learners, we need regular protected time together, time that allows for exploration into the complexity of teaching and learning. A few days at the beginning of the year and one in the middle are not adequate. Scheduling protected, sufficient, and regular time for professional learning must be one of our first priorities if we want collaborative learning groups to flourish.

Facilitative Structures. Good discussions and rich learning in groups seldom happen by chance. Groups rely on structures, protocols, and routines to guide and focus their learning. Such structures ensure that everyone in the group has a voice, the precious time of the group is well spent, sensitive discussions unfold in a safe manner, and attention is directed where it needs to be for learning to move forward. When a group lacks a formal facilitator, such structures, protocols, and routines can help groups self-facilitate.

Common Language. In schools, there is regular talk about teaching, learning, understanding, knowledge, skills, assessment, curiosity, responsibility, and the like. Such words lie at the heart of the educational enterprise. However, we seldom take the time to talk about what we actually mean by each of these words. As a result, two teachers may think they are both teaching for understanding but may be engaged in wildly different practices and getting quite different results. Developing common language around key ideas helps us support one another and our students more effectively while avoiding miscommunication.

Visibility. My colleagues at Harvard Project Zero and I have written much about the importance of visibility and documentation to the learning process. Making our thinking visible allows a group to better understand where each individual is in his or her learning, to avoid assumptions, and to offer a point of connection for others. When we strive to make our thinking visible, we are pushed to engage with ideas and with others in a way that mere "learning about" seldom encourages. Documentation allows a group access to the history of its own learning for the purposes of sharing that learning with others and reflecting on it oneself. Such documentation provides continuity and institutional memory.

Perspective. Some proponents of professional learning communities suggest putting teachers into groups according to grade or subject level. Although this might simplify logistics, it can also be problematic. The members of such groups already see one another with some regularity and may have well-developed roles, positions, and patterns of interaction that are hard to break. These groups also have a common, ready-made work agenda that can get in the way of professional learning. As a result, it can mean that ideas and practices don't get challenged. Everyone accepts that this is just the way we do it, and new ideas fail to get added into the mix. Putting together diverse groups of teachers allows for new perspectives, practices, and ideas while building a sense of collegiality and a shared mission schoolwide.

Something on the Table. It is easy to talk about schooling and issues of teaching and learning without such discussions ever having much influence on what goes on in the classroom. To avoid this problem, we need to bring evidence of student thinking and learning physically to the communal table around which we gather for our learning. This evidence might be a work sample, a video, or notes from an observation. Such evidence helps us de-privatize teaching and grounds our discussions, keeping us focused on student learning. Furthermore, sharing the responsibility for putting something on the table across a group fosters community and commitment.

Action. One of the biggest dangers for any group of learners is that they become talking groups only, discussing ideas without actually putting them into practice. One cannot truly learn about the practice of teaching without taking action and then reflecting on those actions. Book groups are great, but why read books about teaching and learning if we don't plan to put the ideas into action? Every professional learning group needs to have an expectation of action at its core. What will we do? What will we bring back from that doing to reflect upon collectively? What will we do next as a result of our analysis and reflection? At the end of the day, the purpose of professional learning is to affect classroom practice and student learning, and this idea should be built into the group's expectations.

Challenge. A shortcoming of much PD is that it merely introduces new practices for insertion into one's practice—teaching is viewed as just a matter of technique. In truth, teaching is a responsive act that calls upon us constantly to make decisions in the moment. Our thinking and beliefs about learning, teaching, and thinking guide that decision-making process. Rich professional learning should push and challenge our thinking and beliefs, allowing us to achieve greater clarity and understanding in the process. This means in part that our time together with colleagues be full of questioning and exploration. To leave a learning group session slightly unsettled and still thinking is a good thing. Self-satisfaction and complacency are the death of good teaching.

These eight "wants" speak to the ingredients I have found important as I create cultures of thinking for teachers in a school so that those very same teachers may in turn create cultures of thinking for students in their class-rooms. For the most part, these are elements that I try to design at the outset when I am seeking to build a professional learning culture. However, there is a ninth "want" that is perhaps even more crucial to the long-term success of such groups: **effective facilitation.** The facilitator is the person responsible for the ongoing realization and growth of each of the "wants." The facilitator may or may not be involved in making sure each "want" is there at the outset, but he or she will most assuredly help nurture each as the group progresses. The tools David Allen and Tina Blythe provide here in *Facilitating for Learning* will help support that nurturance to its fullest.

I've had the benefit of discussions with David and Tina over the years to help me grow my skills as a facilitator so that I can shepherd each of these "wants" along in the various groups with which I have been involved. In addition, I have had the good fortune to watch both David and Tina facilitate learning groups and have learned from the power of their modeling. They have taught me a great deal about the importance of stepping back so that others can step forward, even as I monitor and guide this process to ensure its effectiveness. I am delighted that they have gathered their wisdom here in this volume to share with others eager to embark on the journey and experience the joys of facilitating learning with colleagues.

—Ron Ritchhart, Senior Research Associate
Project Zero, Harvard Graduate School of Education
Author of *Creating Cultures of Thinking*

Acknowledgments

We would like to acknowledge colleagues who have contributed to our project their perspectives on and expertise in facilitating teacher groups, especially Christopher Barley, Martha Bolivar, Beth Delforge, Alan Dichter, Sarah Fuentes, Heather Labrum, Peter Lapré, David Leo-Nyquist, Terra Lynch, Miriam Raider-Roth, Ron Ritchhart, Marlene Roy, Dawn Samuels, Joseph Schmidt, Debra Smith, Joan Soble, Gene Thompson-Grove, and Daniel Gray Wilson.

We would also like to recognize other colleagues from whom we have learned about collaboration and facilitation: Jaye Alper, Kevin Fahey, Tiziana Filipini, Frances Hensley, Mara Krechevsky, Ben Mardell, Doug McGlathery, Joseph McDonald, Deborah Milligan, Suzanne Ort, Barbara S. Powell, Carla Rinaldi, and Steve Seidel.

PART I

FACILITATING FOR LEARNING

CHAPTER 1

Introduction

This book (as you may have guessed from the title) is about facilitation, and, more specifically, the facilitation of teacher groups within schools. If you have picked it up (either in hard copy or on your e-reader), you are probably an educator who shares our interest in this important and complex work.

The facilitation of teacher groups has been a central part of our work—individually and collaboratively—for nearly 2 decades now. As both facilitators and coaches of facilitators, we have experienced some of the most rewarding moments of our professional lives—and also some of the most challenging. We remain committed to the work not only because it is essential to improving teacher learning and student learning, but because it is essential to our own learning as well.

This book is intended for teachers and other educators (administrators, coaches, teacher educators, staff developers) who facilitate in a range of contexts: faculty meetings, department meetings, professional learning communities, grade-level teams, and inquiry groups, among others. In it, we share our evolving ideas—based on our studies of facilitators and facilitation, as well as on our own experiences and practices—about what makes this work so challenging and so necessary. We provide resources that we hope will help you facilitate groups productively and find deeper personal satisfaction in that work, whether you are a teacher facilitating a group for the first time or an experienced facilitator seeking to develop your skills further.

In this chapter, we address some preliminary questions: Why a new book on facilitation? What kind of group learning are we talking about? Who will facilitate? How do teachers become facilitators of groups? We also describe how the book is organized and relate this book to our earlier work on facilitation of protocols for examining student work and teacher work.

WHY A NEW BOOK ON FACILITATION?

One of the most important shifts in schools in the past 2 decades has been the growing emphasis on collaboration among teachers and other educators. The use of collaborative teacher learning groups has become an increasingly common strategy for professional development and instructional improvement in schools at every level, in the United States and throughout the world (Mehta, 2013; Villegas-Reimers, 2003). These groups include, among others, study groups, inquiry groups, and professional learning communities (PLCs). Traditional structures such as high school academic departments, elementary or middle school grade-level teams, or instructional leadership teams can also function as vehicles for professional learning, in addition to carrying out administrative functions such as scheduling, budgeting, or allocating resources.

The increasing number and variety of such groups reflect a growing recognition that the most effective forms of teachers' professional development are those that emphasize "learning in and from practice" (Ball & Cohen, 1999)—in other words, teachers learning *with* their own colleagues and *within* the ongoing work of their own schools and classrooms. As Linda Darling Hammond (2014) writes: "Productive professional learning [requires] communal engagement in sustained work on instruction over time" (p. 13). In the next section, and throughout the book, we explore what such productive professional learning looks like.

These views offer a counterpoint to the idea that teachers' professional learning (often equated with "training") primarily occurs outside of the school, in teacher preparation programs, inservice workshops, institutes, graduate courses, and so on. Teachers then apply lessons from those sources within their own classrooms and schools. It is a neat model, but perhaps not sufficient for the kinds of professional learning that teaching demands.

To be clear, we are not disparaging the value of these out-of-school learning experiences—indeed, we both are active as instructors and workshop leaders in preservice and inservice programs. Rather, we believe that opportunities for teachers' within-school and with-colleagues learning, mainly in teacher learning groups, can and must be greatly expanded and improved. Considering how to do this requires us to clarify the term *group learning*.

WHAT KIND OF GROUP LEARNING?

Although most groups require facilitation, not every group requires facilitation for learning. In this section, we describe two key features of the kinds of groups/meetings that are the topic of this book. Such meetings (1) focus on professional learning, and (2) use collaboration as the means to achieve professional learning.

Focus on Professional Learning

By professional learning, we mean the kind of learning that helps the members of the group become more effective educators, better able to understand

and support the learning of all the students for whom they are responsible. Professional learning encompasses a wide range of topics and questions, from instructional strategies to assessment of student learning to pedagogical content knowledge.

It may be helpful here to draw a contrast between groups that focus on professional learning and groups that focus on other kinds of goals. Many groups in schools call for skilled facilitation but do not focus on professional learning: a faculty meeting in which colleagues are figuring out how to create time in the daily schedule to implement the district's newly-adopted reading program, for example, or a task force established to review the student disciplinary process, or a committee that is attempting to develop benchmarks for the 4th-grade science curriculum. Such sessions require facilitation, but these kinds of meetings are focused more on task completion than on the learning of the group members.

Of course, these situations could *also* be about learning—completing tasks and professional learning are not mutually exclusive. But more often than not, the urgent needs of completing the task push aside the important but apparently less time-sensitive goal of professional learning. In Chapter 2, we describe more fully this kind of "learning stance" (in contrast to a "task-completion stance"), and in Chapter 9, we explore ways in which facilitators can help groups to repurpose task-oriented or logistics-focused meetings to incorporate opportunities for professional learning.

Use Collaboration

There are many reasons for members of a group to *communicate* with one another—for example, to let colleagues in the same discipline or grade level know when they will be teaching specific content or skills. Other situations call for colleagues to *coordinate* their actions in completing a task—for example, to ensure that everybody makes an important announcement to their classes. And sometimes, teachers need to *cooperate*—for example, to share a limited set of curriculum resources.

Collaborative learning, however, goes beyond communication, coordination, and cooperation. It occurs only when the group achieves learning outcomes that no single member of the group could have arrived at on her own. True collaboration occurs when the group members have a hand in choosing and shaping the kinds of issues, questions, and practices around which they focus their collective learning. The group members collectively, with support from the facilitator, reach new ideas, questions, and practices that are not wholly predictable at the outset of the group's work. This kind of collaborative learning contrasts with the more predictable outcomes of the expert-led workshop that is focused on conveying specific strategies or content. It also differs from the common examples of communication, coordination, and cooperation described above.

WHO WILL FACILITATE?

The proliferation of teacher groups and the expectation that they will support teachers' professional learning have created a critical problem—and a motivating one for this book: Who is going to facilitate all these group meetings?

In some cases, the answer to this question comes from outside the group or school, in the person of a coach or staff developer. Ideally, she will bring not only expertise in the content on which the groups are focused (such as curriculum mapping or analyzing student achievement data), but also experience in group processes and collaborative decisionmaking. But people with such qualifications are not in plentiful supply. Where they are available, it is not always possible for them to work with every group within a school. Nor do schools always (or even often) have the funding to hire them or to sustain the relationship beyond a few meetings.

More and more, the response to the question of who will facilitate learning groups is "teachers." Very often, teachers are asked to be facilitators for the same groups in which they have been, up to this point, participants. This raises another important question: Is it possible to facilitate a group well *without* already having extensive expertise in various group processes and without necessarily being an expert in the content being discussed?

Our answer to this question is "Yes"—though it is a strongly qualified yes. We believe that, with a particular orientation toward the group, its work, and the facilitator's role (an orientation we describe more fully in Chapter 2), as well as a willingness to "learn on the job," most teachers can move into the role of facilitating their colleagues' learning. They will not be "expert" facilitators—especially at first—but they can be effective, even from their initial facilitation efforts, in supporting a group of colleagues to engage in collaborative professional learning.

In making this assertion, we are not denying that groups will be more effectively facilitated by facilitators with well-developed skills. Rather, our pragmatic stance on facilitation is informed by two important factors. The first is the reality identified above: There simply isn't the supply of highly skilled facilitators required to meet the growing demand created by the proliferation of teacher learning groups. If the effectiveness of teacher learning groups depends on expert facilitation, then many groups are doomed to be ineffective.

The second factor has to do with our understanding of facilitation itself: Effective facilitation relies more on learnable skills than on character traits or the natural inclinations of those who serve as facilitators. And these skills develop over time, through practice and reflection—not unlike the process of becoming a classroom teacher: No one assumes that a first-year teacher is an expert educator. Rather, we assume that, as a starting teacher, her knowledge and skills are good enough to support the learning of a classroom full of students, and that student learning will progress even if the teacher has not fully mastered her craft. Her willingness to learn from her experiences, from the feedback and support of supervisors and mentors, and from ongoing professional development will support her in further developing her skills. The same is true of facilitation.

Our pragmatic stance is bolstered by our experiences. We have seen professional collaborative learning thrive in places where expert facilitation is not available. We have seen teachers step into the role and facilitate collegial discussions that foster professional learning. With teachers like these in mind, as well as other educators (administrators, staff developers, coaches, and so forth) who have more experience facilitating learning groups, we view facilitation as a *trajectory* of experience, from initial, exploratory efforts to more seasoned ones to expert ones. Facilitators at every point along the trajectory can be effective in supporting professional learning within the group(s) they facilitate.

HOW DO TEACHERS BECOME FACILITATORS?

One study of new teacher facilitators (Allen, 2016) illustrates the different ways that teachers take up the formal work of facilitation. Here, we share examples of the experiences of just a few educators involved in the study. (The names used are pseudonyms.)

Many teachers become facilitators because administrators ask them to take on the role. Not surprisingly, administrators often select teachers whom they deem respected by their peers. The teacher chosen might be one who others turn to for advice or who would be identified by others as a "rock star" teacher. One principal, when asked who facilitates the PLC meetings in his school, smiled and responded, "The natural born leaders." Ana's experience illustrates this path to facilitation. She was just starting her second year teaching at her Bronx elementary school when her principal informed her that she would be facilitating her grade-level team. Her principal had observed how, more and more often, other teachers on the team looked to Ana for her opinion, asking, "What do you think?" For some teachers, the invitation (or demand) to facilitate comes as a surprise. For another teacher, Maria, a high school Spanish teacher in Queens, the news came at the end of the school year when her principal suggested she attend a summer facilitative leadership institute. "Lo and behold," she reports, "come September, I was facilitating a group." Maria's case is relatively unique, in that the principal had also provided her with resources to support her development as a facilitator.

In other cases, teachers volunteer to facilitate in groups of which they are already part. For example, Henry recognized that the World Languages team at his small Lower East Side high school often seemed to have unused time during its team meetings. He suggested they use the time for "book club" discussions on professional texts of interest to the teachers on the team. Elsa, as a new high school humanities teacher, decided that curriculum planning would be more efficient and effective if teachers worked together, so she started a voluntary team that met after school.

Some teachers already hold leadership roles such as department chair, lead teacher, or instructional coach. Many of these teachers recognize that their work extends beyond leading or coordinating the group and that they also need to facilitate the group's learning. They learn that they must distinguish between meetings (or parts of meetings) that call for, say, decisionmaking, coordination, or supervision, and those that call for grappling with particular questions and challenges that emerge in the classrooms of the group members.

However teachers come to the role, one reason they may find learning to facilitate especially challenging is that almost no one does it full-time. This makes it difficult to find the time to practice facilitation skills, reflect on them, refine them, and deepen one's understanding of the role. Teachers typically spend most of their time on their "real" job: creating lesson plans, evaluating student work, communicating with parents, etc. So usually teachers have to develop facilitation skills "on the side" and "on the fly." We hope this book offers some support for this informal on-the-job learning that most facilitators rely on.

HOW IS THIS BOOK ORGANIZED?

We have organized the book to be useful both as an exploration of the role of facilitating for learning and as a handbook of strategies for enacting the role within teacher learning groups. Though many readers will benefit from the early chapters defining what we mean by facilitating for learning, and the middle ones on the basics of facilitating teacher learning groups, more experienced facilitators may want to jump to later chapters that address particular challenges facilitators (and groups) may encounter within school contexts.

Part I: Facilitating for Learning (which includes this chapter) explores what we mean by professional learning and the idea of taking a "learning stance" toward a group's work. It defines facilitation for learning in terms of key commitments the facilitator makes to the group's learning. It contrasts facilitating for learning with other professional development functions, including staff development, coaching, and supervision.

Part II: Facilitating Teacher Learning Groups: The Basics lays out some of the basic responsibilities and tasks of facilitating teacher learning groups.

These responsibilities and tasks are grouped more or less chronologically, beginning with how the facilitator helps the group prepare for its meeting. Subsequent chapters address supporting the group's learning during the meeting, helping the group close the meeting, communicating with participants after the meeting, and beginning the preparation for the next meeting. For each set of responsibilities and tasks, we share possible facilitation "moves" the facilitator might employ to carry them out.

Part III: Opportunities and Challenges considers some of the challenges facilitators address in working with groups over time. These include challenges related to school culture and leadership, group interactions, and time constraints. It considers ways that facilitators can help groups *repurpose* meetings that are not initially focused on teacher learning (specifically, those meetings where the agenda and outcomes have been set by others outside of the group) so that the meetings can become more learning-focused. Chapters in this part will be more germane to the work of those who already have some experience facilitating groups. However, they also may be of interest to the novice facilitator in looking down the road a bit to the opportunities and challenges that lie ahead. We conclude with perspectives of expert facilitators.

The Appendix includes references to other works on facilitation as resources for all facilitators to continue to develop their facilitation practice.

HOW DOES THIS BOOK RELATE TO
THE FACILITATOR'S BOOK OF QUESTIONS?

Some readers may be familiar with *The Facilitator's Book of Questions*, our first book on facilitation. In that book, we focused on the skills needed to facilitate protocols, or structured conversations for the collaborative examination of student and teacher work. Although protocols often function as key activities within a teacher group's meeting agenda, and thus are an important presence in this book (see Figure 5.1: Protocol Primer in Chapter 5), our scope here extends to encompass broader aspects of the facilitator role, articulating dimensions of the role that were left tacit in the first book. In particular, we focus on the facilitator's responsibilities for supporting a group's learning during all parts of a meeting, and between meetings. We also consider how the facilitator addresses challenges that emerge within a group and within the larger school context and culture.

At the heart of both books is a common mission: to help facilitators support teachers' professional learning in ways that enable everyone to support more powerful student learning.

A NOTE ABOUT TERMINOLOGY

In this book we refer to *teacher* learning groups. We do not mean to suggest that administrators are never part of such learning groups, either on their own (an "administrator learning group") or as part of a learning group of teachers and administrators combined. We use the term simply as an acknowledgment that in most schools such groups are mainly made up of teachers. Similarly, when we focus on teachers-as-facilitators, it is not because we exclude administrators, coaches, staff developers, or others who might facilitate such groups. Again, we are simply recognizing the reality that teachers are increasingly stepping into the role of supporting their colleagues' professional learning in meetings. In fact, we hope the book will be of use to anyone with an interest in and commitment to collaborative professional work and learning in schools.

CHAPTER 2

Facilitating for Learning

We think of facilitating for learning as helping a group take responsibility for, reflect on, and deepen its participants' learning and the learning of their students. It also involves helping the group continually reflect on and improve the processes it uses to support that learning. Taking this definition as the starting point, this chapter explores the term *facilitating for learning* in more depth. First, we consider the "learning" half of the equation. We describe:

- The specific conceptualization (or "story") of professional learning that we think facilitators of teacher learning groups are supporting.
- The kind of intellectual and emotional "stance" that all participants need in order to engage in this kind of collaborative professional learning.

Next, we turn our attention to the "facilitating" part of the definition. Here, we:

- Relate our understanding of facilitation to the way others (in education as well as other fields) have defined that role.
- Identify the key commitments that a facilitator needs to make in order to facilitate for learning.
- Contrast the role of someone who is facilitating collaborative professional learning with the roles of others in the school who are also typically involved in supporting professional development.

DEVELOPING A DIFFERENT STORY OF PROFESSIONAL LEARNING

Being part of a teacher learning group often requires the group's participants to shift their ideas about both the process and products of professional learning. This shift is analogous to a change in classroom culture that educational researcher Ron Ritchhart and colleagues describe. Ritchhart, who for 2 decades has studied and written about the development of "cultures of thinking" in classrooms, describes an intellectual shift that takes place in the classrooms in which teachers are working to nurture a culture of thinking: Students (and their teachers) move from focusing on work production (or assignment completion) to focusing on learning and thinking. This does not mean students stop carrying out tasks; it does mean that the tasks they do are designed to support and reveal critical aspects of their thinking (Ritchhart, Church, & Morrison, 2011).

Ron Ritchhart asserts that, in such "thinking-oriented" classrooms, students (most of whom are accustomed to "work-oriented" classrooms) need to develop a new and different story about what it means to be a learner. He describes several features of that new story, in contrast to the old, and we adapt those here to delineate the parallel shift that teachers (and administrators) need to make in their own conceptions of professional learning.

The old and familiar story of professional development has these features:

- *Not knowing is a sign of weakness.* After the first few years of teaching, having to ask for help or acknowledging one's challenges in the classroom is tantamount to admitting professional incompetence.
- *Having the answers is essential.* Solving problems is more important than asking questions. A professional development session isn't effective unless it provides strategies and techniques that can be immediately implemented in classrooms.
- *Professional learning, like teaching itself, is primarily about individual effort.* Although teachers might attend workshops and other professional development sessions as a group, the work of implementing the strategies and techniques that are often the focus of such sessions is primarily a solo endeavor. Collaboration with colleagues is nice, and can even be helpful, but it is not essential and is usually too time-consuming to be worth the effort.

The formation and operation of teacher learning groups calls for group members to compose a different story of professional learning, one that contrasts sharply with the old conceptualization. Adapting Ritchhart's ideas about student learning to describe teacher learning, the new story looks something like this:

- *Professional learning is a product of thinking and reflecting, not just "doing the work."* Teachers need time away from the classroom not just for learning new instructional techniques or curriculum content in workshops but also for reflecting on their own and their students' day-to-day activities in the classroom.
- *Professional learning, thinking, and reflection require collaborative as well as individual effort.* In fact, without the perspectives of colleagues, the capacity to reflect productively on one's own teaching and students' learning is sharply limited.

- *Learning about teaching and learning involves uncovering complexity and delving deeply.* It can't be made simple. Workshops and courses provide important sources of information and food for thought; however, there is no substitute for studying and analyzing the day-in, day-out work that is taking place in one's own classroom. Doing so involves framing thoughtful questions about the learning of one's students and one's own instruction, and using samples of student and teacher work as data for pursuing those questions.
- *Professional learning is often provisional and changes with time.* The complexity of teaching demands that conceptualizations of and solutions to important problems need to be continually revisited and revised. Issues that seemed straightforward at earlier points in one's career become more complex and problematic over time. Rethinking the ideas and strategies that one has always taken as "givens" is an essential part of professional learning.
- *Professional learning is an active process and involves getting personally involved.* Professional learning of the most thoughtful kind involves acknowledging uncertainty, questioning assumptions, airing frustrations, and taking risks—all deeply personal and emotion-laden acts, especially when carried out in the company of colleagues. In short, it is impossible to take the personal—and interpersonal—out of professional learning.
- *Questions not only drive professional learning but are also outcomes of that learning.* Generating strategies that can be implemented immediately in the classroom is important. Just as important is the process of generating questions—for example, about what supports a student needs in order to learn or how particular curriculum content is most effectively introduced to students. Framing and exploring these questions can lead both to the limits of one's understanding and to the next opportunities for learning. Rather than being an admission of incompetence, saying "I don't know" or "I'm not sure" is the starting point for deeper exploration and the further development of expertise.

At its heart, then, facilitating for learning is about helping group members deepen their understanding of not only their students' learning but also what it means to learn professionally and collaboratively.

A TALE OF TWO STANCES: TASK COMPLETION AND LEARNING

To help this new story of professional learning take root, facilitators can encourage participants to resist the pull of the "task-completion stance," helping them instead cultivate a "learning stance." Right away, we want to make a distinction between *completing tasks* and a *task-completion stance*. Completing tasks is an essential function of what teachers do, either individually or in groups: creating lesson plans and assessments, evaluating student work, aligning curriculum units with established standards and benchmarks, and so on. All these activities are important, and all can be undertaken with either a task-completion stance or a learning stance. A central and ongoing purpose in the facilitator's work is to create conditions that foster a learning stance—even when completing a task is central to or inherent in the purpose for the group's work.

A task-completion stance highlights the finished product. When this stance is operating, one might expect to hear comments such as "Let's get it done," or "Let's push through this," or "Check. What's next?" A learning stance, in contrast, inflects the group's activity with an emphasis on asking questions, seeking explanations, trying out possible solutions, and so on. When a learning stance is operating, we expect to hear questions such as "What do we need to understand in order to carry out this task?" or "What are some other possible explanations for . . . ?" or "What's your evidence for . . . ?"

We relate a learning stance to the *inquiry stance* described by Cochran-Smith and Lytle (2009) as one that "involves a continual process of making current arrangements problematic, questioning the ways knowledge and practice are constructed, evaluated, and used; and assuming that part of the work of practitioners individually and collectively is to participate in educational and social change" (p. 121). At the heart of both inquiry and learning are the questions that drive our actions and reflections—and that should provide the organizing focus for our discussions and meetings.

With so much on their plates, individually and collectively, it is natural that teachers and teacher groups might enter into a situation with the task-completion mindset of solving a problem or finishing a product, and then moving on. The problem with a task-completion stance is that it diminishes possibilities for learning. It encourages individuals or a group to exclude alternative possibilities or perspectives because these will slow down the work. But, as Dewey (1934) argued—and as educators know all too well—learning is neither linear nor orderly. It involves "a rhythm of seeking and finding, of reaching out for a tenable conclusion and coming to what is at least a tentative one" (p. 186). This, of course, takes more time than simply getting things done—and time is always at a premium in schools (a challenge for groups and facilitators that we explore in Chapter 10).

A learning stance is equated with being *process*-oriented as opposed to *product*-oriented. However, a learning stance does not mean that a group does not create products. In fact, John-Steiner (2000) identifies "jointly chosen products" as one of the key characteristics of creative collaboration. It does mean that the precise dimensions of those products, or outcomes, are not known at the outset. The group, with the support of the facilitator, determines the questions it will pursue and the tools (activities, protocols, and so forth) it will use to pursue them. These questions and tools in turn shape the products that emerge, whether they are instructional strategies, assessment techniques, inquiry questions, analytical categories for students' work, or others.

Even when the expectations for the product of a group's work are pretty clear from the outset (for example, developing a common assessment or analyzing the results of a standardized test), it is possible to engage in a process that supports learning. In Chapter 9, we consider how the facilitator can help groups turn such product-oriented tasks into learning opportunities—and still complete the assigned tasks.

Learning and getting things done are not mutually exclusive; however, the impulse to solve a problem or create a product quickly and then move on to the next problem or product (hallmarks of a task-completion stance) can constrain opportunities for learning. Facilitation plays a significant role in how completing tasks (or, better yet, addressing questions) can activate and promote learning—learning about students, instruction, assessment, content, and more.

DEFINING FACILITATING FOR LEARNING

We define facilitating for learning this way: Helping a group take responsibility for, reflect on, and develop ideas for deepening its participants' learning and improving the processes the group uses to support that learning. Our definition of facilitating for learning is informed by studies of facilitation as practiced in schools as well as research and practice in social work, community activism, and business.

The facilitation literature describes a range of purposes and functions for the role: empowering participants to learn (Heron, 1999); promoting participation, ensuring equity, and building trust (McDonald et al., 2013); encouraging full participation, promoting mutual understanding, fostering inclusive solutions, and cultivating shared responsibility (Kaner, 2007); and engaging participants in active learning, informing the group with relevant knowledge, involving the group in active participation, and planning for future applications (Brooks-Harris & Stock-Ward, 1999).

Across these definitions, a core feature emerges: *creating conditions that encourage participation and learning.* To facilitate well, facilitators must encourage the participation of all members of the group. They must diagnose problematic situations as they arise and intervene in ways that will maintain a positive, productive working climate. And facilitators must support interactions that promote the group's learning—recognizing that learning takes many forms, from problem solving to deep inquiry into problems of practice.

One point where we differ from at least some other researchers is the involvement of the facilitator in the content, as well as the process, of the group's work. Schwarz (2002) describes the facilitator as the "substantively neutral person who is not a group member and who works for the entire group" (p. 8). Our pragmatic definition of a facilitator does not exclude a teacher or other educator who also participates in the group from playing the role of facilitator—if it did, many teacher groups would go without any facilitation at all. Here again, one can compare the facilitator of a group to the teacher with her students—if one conceives of the entire class as a learning group, then the teacher is also a member of that group (Krechevsky & Mardell, 2001).

Our definition does describe a person who plays a unique role within the group in terms of her attention to process, as well as learning—a role that needs to be recognized by the group and the person playing it. Ideally, the facilitator should also be acknowledged publicly by the school's administration.

What, then, does the facilitator need to do in order to help a group to take responsibility for, reflect on, and develop ideas for improving its own process? In our view, the facilitator's work begins with cultivating a specific orientation toward the group's work and her own.

THE FACILITATOR'S ORIENTATION

We use the term *facilitator orientation* to refer to the set of attitudes or dispositions that a facilitator of collaborative professional learning brings to his work. The facilitator's orientation is separate from (though linked to) facilitation skills—a term we use to designate strategies, moves, and use of tools (activities, protocols, and so on) and resources—all the things a facilitator *does* in order to help a group to work thoughtfully toward developing deeper professional learning (many of which we review in Chapters 3 through 7). The orientation is not about *what* the facilitator does but *why* and *how* she does it.

The facilitator's orientation comprises three central commitments. These commitments, more than any particular set of skills, are what enable a teacher, or any educator, to be an effective facilitator for a collaborative learning group.

- *A commitment to making the group's goals and process explicit, transparent, and equitable.* The facilitator helps the group become and remain conscious of its goals and process for reaching the goals. She invites the group's reflection on that process at each stage of the work. This doesn't mean that the group will never be caught in the uncertainty of not knowing which direction to take: Moments of ambiguity or even floundering frustration are part of every true collaborative learning process. When the group process falters or the goals become unclear (or even contradictory), it's not so much the facilitator's job to fix the problem as it is to call the group's attention to it and invite the group to reflect on the problem and ways to address it.

- *A commitment to allowing the group's learning outcomes to emerge from the group members and their work together over time.* The facilitator strives to create conditions for the group to determine which questions it will examine rather than trying to steer the group toward a set of preconceived outcomes. Creating conditions for outcomes to emerge is far from passive waiting. Rather, it demands asking thoughtful questions, close (or "active") listening, "replaying" what the facilitator hears, and a host of other skills. It also requires a degree of comfort with ambiguity as well as a sense of when to press the group to make a decision, narrow its focus, move on to the next activity on the agenda or the next step of the discussion protocol, and so forth. As we discuss in the next section, this aspect of the facilitator's role distinguishes the facilitation of collaborative professional learning from the work of a trainer or workshop leader, as well as from that of a coach, mentor, or supervisor.

- *A commitment to one's own learning about learning.* The facilitator needs to reflect on her own understanding of how learning occurs. What are her assumptions about how people learn as a group? About how groups develop? About how learning occurs over time? All educators have tacit theories about these things. Being an effective facilitator of collaborative professional learning means figuring out how to articulate these tacit theories as explicitly as possible—and to reflect on and revise them as necessary. This ongoing reflection occurs individually, with group(s), and, whenever possible, with other facilitators. In Chapter 1, we saw some examples of beginning facilitators' reflections on the role; in Chapter 11, we share those of expert facilitators.

These commitments are challenging to many educators, especially those of us who have experienced professional development mainly as a delivery of information or a training-up in a specific instructional strategy or approach. They become clearer in considering how the facilitator's role is different from that of others concerned with professional development and instructional improvement.

FACILITATION AND OTHER ROLES

We have worked with many coaches, administrators, staff developers, trainers, department chairs, and grade-level coordinators who have wisely and effectively played the role of facilitator for learning when a group's purpose called for them to do so. Facilitating in general, and facilitating for collaborative professional learning in particular, is often part of the work with which these roles

are typically charged, but it is certainly not the only part. Therefore, it is crucial to be clear about how facilitating for learning differs from other professional roles these individuals play.

The work of facilitating collaborative learning requires a fundamentally different orientation from other kinds of work carried out by people holding such roles. Coaches, trainers, staff developers, and department or grade-level chairs often have clear products or end points in mind when they begin work with an individual or group. For example, the goal might be to help the individual or a group learn a certain instructional technique or assessment strategy, or to implement a particular curriculum. With clear goals established, the coach or department chair then leads group activities and discussions with the aim of helping the participants achieve those particular goals.

By contrast, when someone is serving as a facilitator of collaborative professional learning, she takes the group's process as her main focus. The specific outcomes of the group's work are usually much less clear at the outset of the group's work than they would be for someone in the other roles listed above. Indeed, the facilitator of the group may need to work hard initially to keep both the group and herself from leaping too quickly to specifying the exact outcomes toward which the group should be working, recognizing that such a rush to specificity often comes at the expense of opportunities for learning. For example, the facilitator for learning may suggest a brainstorming activity to help determine a focus question for its upcoming meeting rather than accept one (perhaps more vocal) individual's suggestion.

In a group that is being well facilitated to support collaborative group learning, no one can predict the precise outcome(s) ahead of time. Rather, the person in the facilitation role attends to the *process* the group is using: Is the process inclusive? Is it supporting group members in asking challenging questions? Does it allow for multiple points of view to be heard and considered (Breidenstein, Fahey, Glickman, & Hensley, 2012)?

This kind of facilitation and this kind of group learning begin without prescribed outcomes; however, that does not mean that no outcomes or products are planned. As we noted above, the question a group identifies as a focus and the process (activities, protocols, and so on) it uses to address it are critical in shaping the learning outcomes that will emerge. The facilitator plays a central role in helping the group to identify these questions, which, in turn, profoundly affect the work of the group—and, thus, its outcomes.

FACILITATING TEACHER LEARNING GROUPS: THE BASICS

CHAPTER 3

Preparing for the Meeting

A central concern of the facilitator of a teacher learning group is clarity: supporting the learning group in being clear about its goals and the processes it uses to achieve those goals. Thoughtful preparation is the key to achieving this clarity. To prepare for a meeting, a facilitator engages in (and supports the group's engagement in) the following tasks:

- Identify goals.
- Shape the agenda.
- Prepare space and materials.

As with all aspects of facilitation, the amount of time this preparation takes and the best way to do it depend heavily on the group's context. The process of identifying goals is particularly sensitive to context: Groups will engage with this work differently depending how long the group has been together, how long it will continue to meet, whether some portion of its work is being mandated by people outside of the group, and other considerations.

The facilitator's responsibilities and the lists of possible moves she can use in carrying them out might seem daunting at first. Remember: None of these responsibilities rests solely on the facilitator, though the facilitator is the one who might need to do the work to get others involved in sharing those responsibilities. And if time is tight, keep in mind that even a small amount of preparation time, thoughtfully spent, can yield sizable benefits in terms of the focus and depth of the group's work.

That said, if for some reason you absolutely *had* to facilitate a meeting without having had the chance to prepare, there are ways of handling that situation that can still support the group's learning—see Chapter 4 for ideas about constructing an agenda on the spot.

IDENTIFY GOALS

Identifying goals might be the single most important facilitation responsibility discussed in any of these chapters. A group's goals answer the simple—and absolutely essential—questions: Why are we here? Why does this group exist?

If the goals are clear and compelling to everyone in the group and are revisited regularly, they can help the group stay motivated in the face of difficulties, make thoughtful choices about week-to-week activities, gauge progress accurately, and adjust course as needed.

Different Levels of Goals

Teacher learning groups usually need two levels of goals: The first level includes the overarching goals that spell out the learning and work that the group aims to accomplish over the long term. The second level comprises more specific and discrete goals that guide the group's meetings and activities from week to week. Consider the following examples.

For a middle school collaborative inquiry group focused on the assessment of writing, long-term goals might include addressing the following questions:

- Why are our students not showing stronger skills when it comes to editing their own writing?
- How can our assignments and assessment strategies support students in becoming better editors of their own writing (while also making sure that the assessment strategies are actually do-able, given our class sizes and limited planning time)?

Short-term goals for a specific meeting or series of meetings might include:

- Survey current assessment practices.
- Decide what data to collect in order to understand the relative strengths and weaknesses of those practices (samples of student writing, student scores on writing rubrics, interviews with or surveys of students, and so forth).

For a high school math department, long-term goals might include answering questions such as these:

- Why are so many of our students still scoring so low on the state's math assessment when we have significantly increased time on task in all the math classes in the past 3 years?
- What will help us better understand our students' math struggles and what can we do to respond?

More meeting-specific goals for the same team might include:

- Examine a broad sampling of student work to look for patterns in the difficulties students are having.

- Conduct a careful analysis of what "time on task" looks like in various classrooms.

Often, the long-term goals, framed as questions, provide the opportunity and impetus for the group's learning. Divorced from these larger questions, the more specific, task-level goals take on the quality of mere activities to be completed and checked off a list, generating no deeper understanding or cumulative learning for the group's members. For the group to be a teacher *learning* group, at least one or two of the group's long-term goals need to invite the group into an *inquiry* or exploration of some kind. (For this reason, we prefer to frame long-term goals as questions rather than as statements. Some groups also choose to frame their meeting-level goals as questions in order to keep the emphasis on learning even as the group carries out specific tasks.)

Of course, the world is an imperfect place: For various reasons, you might find yourself facilitating a group that is *called* a "teacher learning group" (or a "professional learning community" or a "study group") but that has been assigned a very particular task (to align the school's science curriculum with the state standards, perhaps, or to develop the timeline for preparing students to take the new end-of-year standardized tests)—with no actual learning goal in sight. If this is your situation, head for Chapter 9, where we share some suggestions for ways to support a group's learning under such circumstances.

Developing Long-Term Goals

Teacher learning groups take different forms. Some groups are focused on a single goal, shared equally by all members. In other groups, each member has his or her own learning goal, and group members support one another in working toward their individual goals. Still other groups are formed to carry out a specific task on behalf of their department or school and then develop related learning goals of their own to pursue in conjunction with accomplishing that task. In all of these cases, what is critical is that *the members of the group have a role in establishing the goals.*

This agency that groups have to determine the direction of their work and learning is one characteristic that distinguishes teacher learning groups from other kinds of groups. This characteristic grows out of two foundational assumptions about teachers and teaching: (1) As the people who work most closely with students day-to-day, teachers are the ones who, as professional educators, are able to see classroom challenges most clearly and identify the questions and goals that they need pursue in order to address those challenges; and (2) teachers' work lives are already filled to overflowing with demands on their time, intellectual energy, emotional reserves, and physical stamina. Meaningful professional learning demands a level of commitment and effort above and beyond these already intense day-to-day demands. This extra effort is reasonable only if the ultimate goal has deep personal and professional importance to the person or people making the effort.

If you are facilitating a teacher learning group, it may come as a relief to know that it is not up to you to set the long-term goals for the group. On the other hand, it *is* your job to help the group identify its goals. Here we suggest some strategies, which we refer to as *possible facilitation moves*, you might use. Note that most of these strategies are designed for a group that is just forming; however, any of them could be used to help an already-established group revisit, reflect on, and perhaps reformulate its goals.

POSSIBLE FACILITATION MOVES

Invite the group members to do some reflective writing.

What do they hope to accomplish in this group? What do they hope to learn? You might invite participants to respond to such prompts via email or in a Google Doc, or some other electronic way of enabling all participants to see one another's responses. You might also ask them to bring very brief written reflections to a meeting, written large enough (or printed out using a large enough font) that their papers can be taped to the wall and still be easily read by the whole group. This would allow the group to review and discuss the connections and differences among the group members' goals.

Use protocols to help a group identify and refine important inquiry questions.

Protocols are structures for guiding a group's interactions. (For a more complete explanation, see Figure 5.1: Protocol Primer in Chapter 5.) One protocol that is useful for helping teacher learning groups develop an inquiry question is the Choosing a Question Protocol (see Figure 3.1). This protocol can be used either to develop an inquiry question for an individual teacher or for an entire group. It can also be used to "tweak" an inquiry question that does not seem to be working

Articulate a goal first, and then invite people to join the group.

One way to ensure that all group members are invested in the group's goals for both work and learning is to establish the goals of the group first and then invite people who want to pursue such goals to join the group. ("A few of us would like to start a group focused on getting a better understanding of close reading and how to help kids do it. If you're interested, join us for an

Figure 3.1. Choosing a Question Protocol

This protocol helps clarify the process for choosing an inquiry question to focus on. As teachers or groups identify questions about their practice and their students' learning, they are asked to consider the criteria below. If it is an individual question, the presenting teacher addresses the criteria first, followed by other group members. If it is a group question, all members of the group are invited to address the criteria, with perhaps everyone sharing perspectives on each criterion before moving on to the next.

1. Importance: Why is this question personally important to you?
2. Relevance: How is it relevant to teaching and learning in other classrooms?
3. Focus on Student Learning: What direct connections to student learning can you identify?
4. [Optional] Scope: Does the question feel too specific or too broad?

If the group feels that the question meets all the criteria, the question is considered appropriate for inquiry. If a question doesn't meet these criteria, the group considers how the question could be modified—or whether another question might be more appropriate for inquiry.

Developed by the Evidence Project Research Team (adapted from *The Evidence Process*, 2001)

initial meeting in the library after school on Thursday.") This approach may be encouraged in some schools, but difficult to achieve in others. Even when a group is entirely voluntary, it is still important to invite the group members to reflect on and share their personal goals with one another.

Developing Short-Term Goals

Identifying the goals for specific meetings or other group activities is usually relatively easy once the overarching goals are articulated. Often, meeting goals grow directly out of the work of previous meetings: If the group examined student work for evidence of patterns in students' difficulties last week, then this week might be devoted to identifying or developing strategies for addressing the most prevalent student challenges or misconceptions. Again, the facilitator's main job is to invite thoughts from the group, formulate possible meeting goals, and then check the goals with the group—always helping the group keep in mind the larger, overarching goals toward which they are working collectively.

SHAPE THE AGENDA

Having an agenda does not guarantee a productive meeting. Not having one often predicts an unproductive one. Typically, the facilitator is the person in the group responsible for putting together the agenda; however, that should not mean that she is the only person involved in creating it.

Before we discuss strategies or moves for creating a sound agenda, let's consider the purposes an agenda serves. The word *agenda* in Latin means "things to be done." Simply put, an agenda answers the question: What activities will the group try to accomplish in the meeting? It also answers two others: What order of activities will be most efficient and effective? And, given that time is limited, how much time should the group spend on each activity? (Note: In putting together an agenda, it is usually helpful to think and speak in terms of "activities" rather than "items"—a semantic shift that signals a focus on *actions* rather than *things*.)

In developing an agenda, then, the facilitator balances these three essential and interrelated concerns: activities, sequence, and time. A good agenda is also:

- *Goal-oriented.* The agenda translates the group's goals into action. Though there may be items on an agenda that do not have a clear connection to the goals (e.g., reviewing the calendar of upcoming school events or collecting contributions for a colleague's retirement party), as much as possible the core activities should relate strongly to the goals or questions for learning that the group has articulated.
- *"Do-able."* The agenda offers a realistic projection of the actions the group can accomplish, given the allotted time and the available resources. This does not mean that every activity has to be completed within the meeting. Some activities begun in the meeting will need to be continued through what people do between meetings and/or in the next meeting.
- *"Telegraphic."* The format and wording of the agenda provide participants with a clear and concise picture of what the group will do during the meeting (i.e., bullet points, not paragraphs).

Figure 3.2 shows an agenda for a 45-minute teaching team meeting. In addition to listing the group's activities, it has some other features: the group's long-term goals as well as the meeting goals, the time estimates for each activity, and the specific reflection question that the group will address briefly at the conclusion of the meeting (enabling group members to keep it in mind throughout the meeting).

Some useful facilitation moves for creating an agenda follow. In developing an agenda, just as in developing goals, the facilitator serves as a catalyst for the group's thoughts, so you'll see some overlap with the moves outlined in the section above.

Figure 3.2. Sample Meeting Agenda

Eighth-Grade Team Meeting

Agenda, November 5

Big-Picture Goals:

- Understand what the Common Assessment can (and can't) tell us about our students' learning.

- Figure out how to use our analysis to improve instruction.

Today's Goal:

- Decide the criteria we'll use to choose the students' work that we will examine in depth for the next few weeks.

1. Check-in—5 minutes

2. Review agenda and goals for meeting—2 minutes

3. Examine data from Common Assessment (use modified Tuning Protocol)—25 minutes

4. Identify criteria for selecting focal students for discussion—5 minutes

5. Reflect: What are we learning about the strengths and weakness both of our students and of the Common Assessment? (Writing, followed by "whip")—3 minutes

6. Identify next steps—2 minutes

7. Announcements—2 minutes

Some groups post their goals on the wall; others include them on the agenda—a steady reminder of the group's ultimate purposes.

Protocols are tools that are often used within specific parts of meetings to guide the group's discussion. See the Protocol Primer (Figure 5.1) in Chapter 5 for more details.

Announcements have a way of taking up more time than anticipated. Putting them last on the agenda rather than first means that the most essential parts of the meeting are more likely to get the time they need. And if the meeting runs a bit long, the announcements can usually be handled by email or in some other context.

"Check-in" is an opportunity for the group to make the transition from the hectic school day to the more reflective mode of the meeting. Strategies for supporting this transition are described in Chapter 4.

Time estimates help the group make decisions about whether to stay with a topic or move on: If the group decides to give more time to one topic, it's easier to see what will need to get shortened or taken off the agenda altogether.

A "whip" is a group reflection strategy explained in Chapter 6.

POSSIBLE FACILITATION MOVES

*Review notes and documentation from
previous meeting (or meetings).*

What did the group say it was going to do? What activities might be continued or repeated?

Get others' input.

Try to check in, face-to-face or online, with participants to gather their ideas for activities and/or to get feedback on the draft agenda you have already prepared. This can even begin in the last few minutes of the meeting that is wrapping up, simply by asking, "Ideas for the next meeting?"

Do a mental rehearsal of how the meeting will proceed.

Visualize how each activity will begin and end, as well as the transition to the next activity. Try to anticipate what kinds of questions or concerns might emerge that could necessitate adjusting the agenda.

Build in some "wiggle room."

This might mean allocating a few more minutes for each activity than it typically might take, recognizing that at least some activities are likely to take longer than anticipated.

Put it in writing.

Make paper copies of the agenda to distribute at the meeting (Some groups mitigate environmental damage by copying the agenda on half-sheets of paper.) Although it is also possible to post the agenda on chart paper or project an image of it from a computer, paper copies allow everyone to use the agenda (as well as any other information included on it, such as goals and reflection questions) during the meeting and to pencil in any revisions that might be needed as the meeting progresses. It also serves as an artifact for the group's documentation (see Chapter 6).

Share a draft of the agenda with the group in advance.

This is not always possible. When it is possible, getting this round of feedback in advance may enable you to take care of concerns and incorporate ideas that might otherwise need to be handled with some on-the-fly revisions at the beginning of the meeting. These in-meeting revisions are not necessarily problematic, but the less time spent on shaping the agenda in the meeting, the more time the group can spend on the substance of the meeting.

Of course, some agendas are dictated by the group's work plan for the semester or year. Even if certain activities are more or less prescribed (perhaps by the administration or some other body), the facilitator can still help the group consider how these tasks might be accomplished in ways that support the group's learning (see Chapter 9).

PREPARE SPACE AND MATERIALS

Space matters as much for teacher learning as it does for student learning. Having adequate room to work, sufficient lighting, and insulation from distracting movement or loud sounds in the surrounding area all contribute to an environment that supports learning. But schools are rarely equipped with sufficient meeting spaces suitable for teacher learning groups. Many meetings take place in "borrowed" spaces such as the school library or the cafeteria or in a corner of the faculty room. Often, the best bet for a teacher learning group meeting is an empty classroom—but only if the group can take steps to modify the arrangement of the space. Classrooms, usually set up to accommodate 20–35 students, often have desks or tables arranged to face the front of the room. However, the best setup for a teacher learning group is a circle in which each group member can make eye contact with all other members.

To achieve such an arrangement in a classroom (or any other room in a school, for that matter), you usually have to move the furniture. This can be time-consuming, annoying, and even physically difficult. But if you wind up in a space where the setup does not allow for all group members to see, hear, and talk easily with all other group members, then moving the furniture is absolutely essential.

In addition to having certain physical qualities that affect learning, the environment provides subtle but powerful symbolic cues about the kinds of activity that can take place in it—and even the kinds of relationships that can develop among the people. A setup in which group members sit in rows facing the facilitator, who sits or stands in front of the group, suggests that the facilitator is the primary source of information and direction for the group. A setup in which some group members are seated in an inner circle while others are seated outside of this circle conveys the message that some group members are more central to the work than others.

Although both of these fairly typical setups (as well as a number of others) might be fine for workshops or graduate classes, they are problematic when it comes to teacher learning groups. The arrangement of the space for a learning group should mirror the central values and goals of the work: that group members learn from and with one another; that the direction and goals for the work grow out of the members' needs, interests, and experiences; that all participants are expected to contribute to the group's process; and that the facilitator supports the group's learning but does not herself "lead" the group's work (the way a workshop leader leads a workshop, for example). The closer you can get to a circle setup, the better the environment will support the spirit of equitable collaboration and shared responsibility that the group will need in order to learn well together.

Other space issues: Consider proximity to whiteboards, chalkboards, unobstructed walls for hanging chart paper, or other resources that allow the group to capture and display notes publicly as they work. Strive for sufficient "work space"—that is, open space everybody can easily access to lay out documents, samples of student work, snacks, and so on.

POSSIBLE FACILITATION MOVES

Ask for help.

Just because the furniture needs moving or chart paper needs transporting doesn't mean you as facilitator have to do it all yourself. Dealing with the logistics of space and materials is an area ready-made for getting others involved. Most of the other moves listed below can be carried out by any group member—or even another person from the school community who is not a member of the group but would be happy to bring the portable projector down from the third floor on her way out or who could pick up copies of the agenda from the main office and drop them off on her way back from recess duty. In the following moves, we encourage the facilitator to *invite others* to help whenever possible.

Find a meeting space for the next meeting.

Tracking down available space in overcrowded schools is not always a simple task. It can be important to start looking early, especially if rooms are scarce and communication about room availability is not always straightforward. It might also be necessary to plan for a backup space. It might be possible to explore alternative meeting spaces off school grounds—in a café, community center, or perhaps a group member's house or apartment. Even if this is just an occasional occurrence, it can create a stimulating change for the group.

Arrange for technology and other materials.

Arrange for whatever materials and technology might be needed to record and/or project ideas. These resources might include a portable whiteboard and dry-erase markers; flip chart, easel, and markers; a computer and LCD projector; a digital camera; and so on. Generally, teacher groups do not record their meetings on digital audio or video; however, there may be specific segments of a meeting that a group agrees should be recorded for documentation purposes.

Move the furniture.

This is usually done just before the meeting takes place. Group members might arrive a few minutes early to help set up. Or, once the group has convened, you might invite the group to spend the first few minutes putting the room in the appropriate configuration. Aim for a circle or a horseshoe oriented toward a whiteboard or other display space (if the group will be doing substantial work with projected images or chart paper recording). Put seats close enough so that people can easily hear and see one another while still maintaining a little breathing room and space for their own materials. Make sure there is enough common workspace to spread out materials the group will use: handouts, copies of student work, data, assignments, food and drink.

Feed people!

This is especially important if the meeting is being held after school when the group's energy is likely to be low. But even if it is held during a typical middle-of-the-school-day planning period, the opportunity to share cookies and coffee or juice carries important symbolic value for the group's developing community. Often, group members volunteer to take turns bringing food, or everyone pitches in to reimburse someone who picks up coffee or other refreshments for the whole group.

CHAPTER 4

Opening the Meeting

As Carla Rinaldi, the president of the board of the Reggio Children Foundation, once noted, "Good beginnings never end." The expression captures the power of the initial stage of a project or initiative to shape everything that comes after it. This is as true for the start of a single meeting as it is for the launch of a long-term project.

Giving a meeting a thoughtful start takes time. In general, time for teachers to meet is at a premium in schools, so there is often a strong temptation to rush through (or skip entirely) initial steps in order to get to "the work" more quickly. It may help to consider a mantra popular in the business world (another context in which time is scarce and pressure is high): "You can go slow to go fast, or you can go fast to go slow." That is, taking time at the beginning of a project or meeting to establish a good foundation can enable more effective and efficient effort as the project or meeting develops. The reverse is also true: Rushing through the startup stage often leads to problems as the work develops, and the need to address those problems slows down the overall effort.

Not surprisingly, we support the slower and more thoughtful approach to getting meetings started—within the constraints time imposes. Here are the key responsibilities that a facilitator should focus on in order to support "good beginnings":

- Facilitate transition and connection.
- Review goals and agenda.
- Establish or review norms.
- Establish or review roles or functions.

Attending to these aspects of the work usually takes more time for a group that is just getting started than it does for an experienced group. For example, a new group will need to develop norms and might take most of an initial meeting to do this. Once norms are well established, however, a brief review (lasting a minute or two) at subsequent meetings is usually sufficient.

FACILITATE TRANSITION AND CONNECTION

Most teacher groups meet in the midst of or at the end of a hectic (if not downright chaotic) workday. Group members rush in to the meeting from a class or another meeting that has just finished and then dash off to the next class or activity on their schedules as soon as the group's meeting concludes. Even when they are physically present in the room, group members can find it difficult to keep their minds on the conversation at hand when a host of urgent to-do's (preparing for the next class, picking up the copies of hand-outs from the office, finding a place for the students who were absent to take a makeup quiz, scheduling an orthodontist appointment for a son or daughter . . .) is clamoring for attention. This game of mental "Whac-a-Mole," along with the usual (and often total) lack of breathing space in the typical workday, is not conducive to thoughtful professional learning and collaboration with colleagues. Given these conditions, providing a way for teachers to transition to the more deliberate and reflective mode of the learning group is not simply a nice gesture; rather, it is an essential part of the facilitator's work in creating conditions for learning. Group members need the opportunity to settle, connect with one another, and connect to the work at hand.

If the group has moved beyond its first meeting, an additional challenge presents itself: creating meaningful connections with what happened during the previous meeting so that the group's learning and work are cumulative. The intervals between the meetings, whether they last a few days or a few weeks, can sometimes seem like months. Beginning a new meeting by giving group members time to remember and connect with questions, ideas, and action steps generated in previous meetings can help develop the continuity needed to enable the group's learning to build over time.

Keep in mind that the possible facilitation moves described here are offered as a menu of options. You'll need to use your own knowledge of the group and your awareness of the meeting's time constraints to choose one or perhaps two of the moves suggested to help your group negotiate transition and reconnection in the meeting. We have provided estimated times for each of the following moves (some as brief as half a minute, and others as long as 30 minutes) to help you choose which activity or combination of activities would be most suited to opening your group's meeting.

POSSIBLE FACILITATION MOVES

Check-in.

Invite group members to go around the circle and share (briefly) one thing that's on their minds, either from their work in school or from their lives outside of school. Remind the group that this is a time not for discussing but simply for sharing and listening. This exercise not only offers group members the opportunity to settle into the meeting but also gives them a chance to learn something about one another. (Time: 5–10 minutes, depending on group size)

"What I need to set aside for the moment . . . ."

Our colleagues from Cambridge Rindge and Latin School, in Massachusetts, Doug McGlathery and Deborah Milligan, often begin meetings by inviting group members to pair up. They then ask each group member to describe for her partner one thing that's weighing on her mind and that might be a distraction in the meeting. Each partner has 1 minute to share her "distracting challenge" and then concludes by saying, "I'm going to try to set this aside for the next 50 minutes [or however long the meeting is]." (Time: 3–5 minutes)

"I remember . . . ."

Ask the group to reflect briefly and quietly on the previous meeting. (You might give the group 20–30 seconds of quiet time to do this.) Then invite group members to share one thing they remember from that meeting. These descriptions should be brief and should not be accompanied by any explanation of why the moment was so memorable—just a sentence-long description of something someone said or did that stands out for them. For example, "I remember Maria shared a sample of her students' geometry projects," or "I remember that we talked about peer-to-peer sharing as a way to give students more discussion time in our classrooms." You might want to remind the group that this is not a time for discussing these particular memories in depth but rather an opportunity to launch the current meeting by creating a collective picture of what transpired at the last one. (Time: 1–3 minutes)

Review documentation.

Documentation is the word we use to describe the tangible artifacts generated at or just after a meeting that capture important aspects of that meeting. (See Chapter 6 for more about documentation.) Such artifacts might include meeting minutes, participants' written reflections on the meeting, or photos taken of the participants as they work together in the meeting. Share this documentation with the participants at the beginning of the meeting, and then invite everyone to offer (briefly) an idea or question that emerges for them as they examine the documentation (or perhaps an idea or question that has come up for them in the interval since the last meeting and that connects to something in the documentation). If time is short, this same exercise can be done in pairs. (Time: 5–10 minutes as a whole group; 3–5 minutes in pairs)

Review action steps.

Often, meetings generate tasks to be completed outside of the meeting, and usually these steps are captured in meeting minutes or an email sent out to participants after the meeting (see Chapter 7). Taking time to review these action steps at each meeting helps ensure continuity for the group's work and recognition of group members who agree to take on tasks. If the tasks are relatively discrete and straightforward (such as reserving a room for a future meeting or tracking down and sharing a specific resource), this review of action items might actually be accomplished via an email exchange a day or two before the meeting. However, if the action steps are more complex (for example, all participants agree to try a particular kind of activity in their classrooms), then it is important to reserve meeting time to review and discuss the results of those efforts. (Time: 3–30 minutes, depending on action steps generated in previous meeting)

Allow a moment to breathe.

Even if meeting time is very limited, it is possible to support participants' transition into the meeting by inviting everyone to sit quietly for 30–60 seconds, taking a few deep breaths. At the end of the allotted time, welcome the group members to the meeting and move into the next part of the agenda. (Time: 1 minute or less)

REVIEW GOALS AND AGENDA

In Chapter 3, we discussed the process of developing both long-term and meeting-specific goals with a group, as well as the process of shaping an agenda with the group's input. If you have gone through those initial preparations, it can be tempting to think that another review of the group's goals and the meeting agenda is a waste of precious meeting time. But consider the fact that even sharing a draft agenda ahead of time doesn't guarantee that everyone has read it with equal care or that everyone fully understands it.

In general, one of the most challenging aspects of group-work (for facilitators as well as other group members) is understanding and making room for the varieties of experience that group members can have in the group simply because they are individuals who have different ways of engaging with and making sense of the world (not to mention the learning group's work). The agenda that sparkles with clarity for one group member may seem somewhat obscure or off track to another. Building a collective understanding of the group's goals and process is not a one-time activity: It is ongoing work. Reviewing the agenda (and how it relates to the group's long-term and immediate goals) is an important step in that ongoing work.

POSSIBLE FACILITATION MOVES

Review agenda and goals with the group.

Hand out hard copies of the agenda and walk the group briefly through the activities. If the agenda itself doesn't make it clear, be sure to explain how the activities relate to the group's overarching goals. If time permits, you might even ask the group to identify the connections they see between the work of this meeting and the larger goals for the learning group. Ask the group if anyone has questions or concerns. After addressing these, move on to the next item.

Construct the agenda with the group in the first few minutes of the meeting.

Preparation before the meeting is usually the most reliable way to ensure a productive meeting. But life intervenes: Snowstorms cancel three days of school. Sons and daughters catch the chicken pox. Avalanches of unexpected paperwork (due tomorrow) cascade down from the central office. And the next thing you know, your carefully reserved prep time has evaporated, the next teacher learning group meeting is upon you, and the agenda has not been prepared. Rather than cancel a meeting that is likely to be difficult to reschedule, you might simply take the first few minutes of the meeting to construct the agenda with the group. Begin with a reflection (perhaps 2 minutes or so) on the last meeting: What do people remember? What action steps or decisions were agreed upon? What issues were left hanging? Then invite suggestions for the present meeting for another couple of minutes: What things should we try to accomplish today? Finally, after reminding the group of the overarching goals, ask the group to nominate priorities: Which activities are the most important for the group to address today? (For efficiency's sake, if there is disagreement in the group, you should feel free, in your capacity as facilitator, to serve as the tiebreaker.)

ESTABLISH OR REVIEW NORMS

Every group has norms, whether those norms have been explicitly identified or not. Norms are the understandings the group members hold about how they work together and communicate with one another. For example, you may have had the experience of being part of a group whose meetings always start late—you know it's fine if people show up 5 minutes late, because nothing is going to happen before then. Probably, no one at the meeting has said, "We should always start late," but that is an *implicit* norm of the meeting. Similarly, you may have been part of a group in which questions that challenge the status quo are not welcome. No one has explicitly stated that such questions should not be asked; however, most group members are acutely aware (or even worried) that these kinds of questions, if raised in the meeting, would lead to unproductive conflict or defensiveness. The implicit norm is, "We should avoid difficult issues"—usually a counterproductive norm if the group's goals are related to improving teaching and learning.

Rather than relying on implicit norms, teacher learning groups need explicit norms designed to support the group's ability to engage in thoughtful collaborative work and learning. These norms serve as guidelines and reminders for group members about how to engage with one another during and between meetings. Norms often address several different aspects of the group's work:

- *Logistics*: to ensure efficiency and effectiveness. For example: "We will start and end meetings on time."
- *Group interactions:* to ensure equitable participation and safety for all group members. For example: "We will make sure everyone's voice is heard." "We will maintain confidentiality about what's discussed in the meeting."
- *Individual differences:* to accommodate unique attitudes or orientations. For example: "We will strive to cultivate curiosity about others' perspectives, especially when they're different from ours."

Often, a group's norms express the group's highest aspirations for working together in the most thoughtful, attentive, and productive ways. As a facilitator, you might be tempted to save time by providing a list of norms for the group and simply asking everyone to agree to it. However, the norms are more likely to be personally meaningful (and therefore more likely to be adhered to) if everyone participates in generating them—including the facilitator.

POSSIBLE FACILITATION MOVES FOR
DEVELOPING GROUP NORMS

If the group is just getting started, the process of developing norms might take a good portion of your first meeting and might also involve a follow-up conversation at your second meeting.

Develop norms based on participants' previous experiences.

Invite group members to reflect on previous groups of which they have been a part and to identify one group that seemed to be particularly effective at accomplishing its goals and supporting the learning of its members. What made that group so effective? What norms did the group follow (or seem to follow, if the norms were implicit)? You might give everyone 2 or 3 minutes to do some reflective writing using these prompts. Next, invite group members to share one norm they identified (and to listen carefully to one another so as not to repeat a norm once it has been articulated). Record the list on chart paper, allowing group members to ask clarifying questions as needed. If the generated list is very long, invite group members to suggest ways to combine norms that seem similar. Usually, four to eight norms are sufficient. (Time: 15–30 minutes, depending on group size)

Develop norms based on participants' hopes for the group's work.

Ask participants to write for a few minutes about what they hope will happen during the group's collaborative work: What would make this one of the most powerful and effective learning experiences of their professional careers? Allow time for each group member to share thoughts. Then ask: "What norms should we follow to help us achieve these aspirations?" (Time: 15–30 minutes, depending on group size)

Work with an already-developed list of norms.

Although norms work best if developed by the group, you might "jump-start" the conversation by bringing in sample norms from other groups. (See Figure 4.1 for an example of a group's norms.) Participants can identify the ones that they think might be useful for the group's work and offer additional norms that are not represented on the sample lists. (Time: 15–30 minutes, depending on group size)

Figure 4.1. Sample Norms for a Middle School Collaborative Inquiry Group

Creating a safe and equitable space

- We will show respect for one another in our interactions in and outside of the meeting.
- We will "share the air," making room for everyone to participate.

Pushing for deeper understanding

- We will acknowledge our uncertainty when we feel it.
- We will take the risk to voice new ideas and to raise challenging/difficult questions.

Managing our time

- We will start and end our meetings on time.
- We will set an agenda and do our best to stick to it.

Handling disagreements

- Respectfully, we will voice our disagreements (not just our agreements).
- When we disagree, we will ask questions in order to better understand the other's perspective.

POSSIBLE FACILITATION MOVES ONCE NORMS ARE ESTABLISHED

Ask group members to commit to the norms.

Once the norms are articulated, all group members should make an explicit commitment to observing them. This commitment can be expressed quickly and easily by asking for a show of hands at the meeting at which the norms are developed. Or you can allow for a more deliberative process by sending the list to the group via email after the meeting, inviting a response either by email or at the subsequent meeting. It is often helpful to invite the group to consider this first version of the norms a draft—one that the group will revisit and revise over time (see suggestions below). (Time: 2 or 3 minutes, if done in the meeting)

Talk about how to handle situations in which the norms are not observed.

Norms encourage everyone to maintain a heightened awareness of the group's process and their own role in it—a level of awareness that is not typical of day-to-day interactions. So it is not surprising that group members, even those who are enthusiastic about the norms and are committed to them, will sometimes fail to observe them. It can be very useful to acknowledge this simple truth when the norms are established and then to ask group members how they would like to be informed if others see that they are not adhering to the norms.

Some groups agree on a nonverbal signal (such as raising a colored card) that members can use when they're concerned that a norm has gone unheeded and would like to call for a pause to discuss it. Or a group might designate one or two of its members to serve as "norm minders," who keep an eye on meeting interactions in relation to the norms and then share their reflections at the end of each meeting. (See the Establish or Review Roles or Functions section below.) (Time: 3–5 minutes)

Review and revise norms.

Holding an initial conversation or two with the group about norms will get the group's work off to a good start. In order to continue to support thoughtful collaboration, norms need to be revisited (and perhaps revised) at regular intervals. At the most basic level, group members need to be reminded of the norms. Some groups include the norms on the same sheet of paper on which the agenda is printed. Others post them in the room. After a few weeks (or a few meetings), invite the group to reflect on the norms: Which norms are the group members observing fairly well? Which ones need tweaking or revising? Are additional norms needed? You might ask participants to reflect on their individual participation as well as on the group's functioning as a whole. (Figure 4.2 provides a sample resource that can be used in this kind of reflection.)

Figure 4.2: Reflection on Group Norms

Consider how you as an individual group member are practicing the norms and how we as a group are practicing the norms. Please share your thoughts using the grid below.

	1–2 norms being successfully practiced	1–2 norms NOT being successfully practiced
Me		
Us		

Suggestions for improvement (revising, deleting, adding norms)?

Adapted from *Arts PROPEL: A Handbook for Music* (1992)

ESTABLISH OR REVIEW ROLES OR FUNCTIONS

In *The Facilitator's Book of Questions* (see Appendix: Resources), we described three kinds of facilitation that are necessary for starting and sustaining teacher learning groups (see Figure 4.3):

- Facilitating *learning*: supporting group members in deepening their learning as they are engaged in their work, both during and outside of the meeting.
- Facilitating *logistics*: addressing the nuts-and-bolts needs of the group—scheduling, meeting space, and so on.
- Facilitating *longevity*: working, often at an institutional level, to help sustain an initiative or a project over time.

Figure 4.3: Facilitating Learning, Logistics, and Longevity

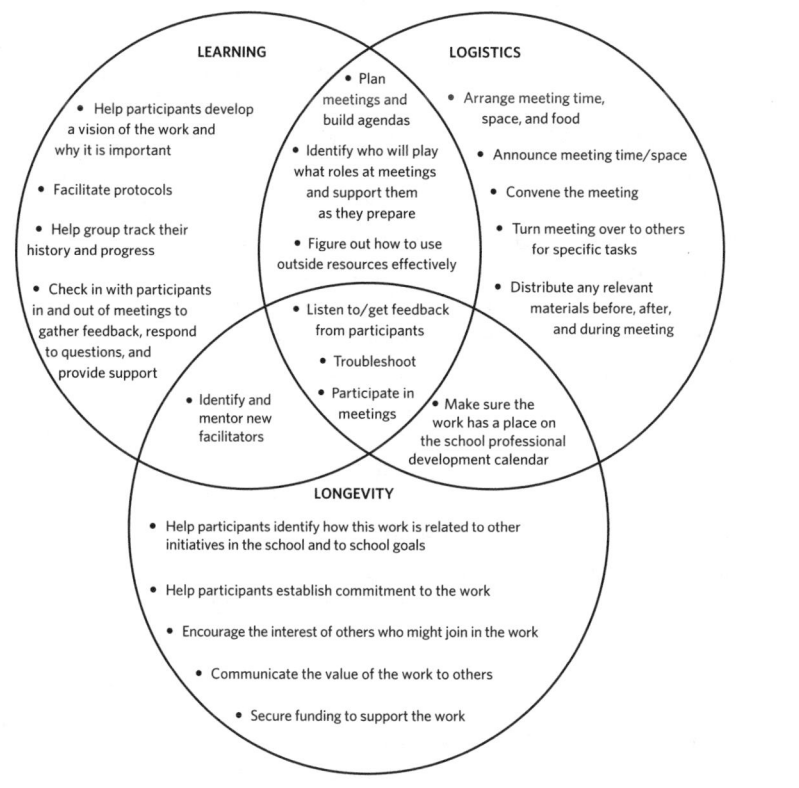

Adapted from *The Facilitator's Book of Questions*, 2004.

In laying out this framework, we stressed the importance of collaboration and shared responsibility at the facilitator level. Rarely is a single person able to carry out all the responsibilities associated with each of these areas. More often, successful initiatives are sustained by collaboration among a number of people, each engaged in a different kind of facilitation: One teacher might serve as a regular facilitator during the meeting (facilitating learning); another teacher might act as the logistics facilitator; a principal or director of professional development might focus on facilitating the longevity of the work.

What are the various functions that need to be served in order for a group to accomplish its tasks and support its learning? In this section, we unpack in more detail the kinds of work involved in facilitating *learning*. It is possible to talk about these responsibilities in terms of roles—having a meeting facilitator, a note-taker, a timekeeper, and so forth. However, we recognize that more often than not, especially if the group is small, such roles will be rotated among group members, and one group member might perhaps take on two or three different roles in a meeting. We talk about "functions" rather than "roles" in order to allow for and encourage this kind of flexible thinking about sharing responsibility for the meeting facilitation. Key functions include the following:

Facilitating. The facilitator is often the person who convenes the meeting, helps the group establish the agenda, and then supports the group's process throughout the meeting in order to ensure clarity of purpose, equity, and safety, thus enabling everyone to participate substantively.

Timekeeping. For very small groups, this function is sometimes accomplished with the use of a smartphone timer. If a person has taken on this role, typically she is asked to signal the facilitator and/or group several minutes before the end of each portion of the meeting so that the group can transition smoothly to the next.

Documenting. Documenting, in this context, means collecting and generating artifacts that capture both what happens in the meeting as well as what participants have learned. Sometimes this function is given the title of "note-taker" or "recorder." In a teacher learning group, documentation captures both what topics were addressed and what the group is learning in the process. This often involves asking participants to reflect on and write about their ideas and questions at the end of the meeting (see Chapter 6 for more about this function).

Backup (or "pinch-hit") facilitating. Facilitating a discussion while also participating in the content of the discussion is challenging. When the person serving as facilitator needs to be involved more substantively in the content of the conversation, she hands the facilitation baton to someone who takes over facilitation duties for that portion of the meeting. Usually, when that portion of the meeting is over, the original facilitator resumes the facilitation responsibilities.

Norm minding. Sometimes, groups ask one or two members to take on the role of monitoring how well the group is observing its norms. When groups do this, they usually also leave time at the end of the meeting for the norm minder(s) to report back to the group on strengths and struggles in the group's observation of its norms. If a group decides to assign this function, usually it is on a rotating basis, with a different member or two serving as the norm minders each time the group meets.

POSSIBLE FACILITATION MOVES

Discuss functions with the group.

The discussion of functions and responsibilities within the meeting might arise naturally in the conversation about norms. If it doesn't, you might simply describe these functions to the group and ask group members to share their thoughts about these or other functions or roles that might be useful for the group—perhaps as they have seen them operate in other meetings. (Time: 5–7 minutes)

Decide with the group whether to assign permanent roles or rotate functions.

The benefit of rotation is that many people get to share in the responsibilities that contribute to productive collaboration. Rotation might happen every meeting, or the rotations might be longer term (with people carrying out their roles for a quarter or a semester). For larger groups, two or three people might rotate each function throughout the year. One drawback of rotating functions, especially if the rotations are frequent, is that group members don't get enough practice to develop real expertise or skill in an area (such as facilitation or documentation). Allowing more time between rotations might help mitigate this.

Ultimately, the point is not to get bogged down in who is playing which role or serving which function, but to carry out these functions in ways that support the group's work and participants' learning.

CHAPTER 5

Working Through the Meeting

Once the meeting is under way, the facilitator's responsibilities are usually pretty straightforward. They involve keeping track of time (or making sure someone else is doing so) and guiding the group in making transitions from one activity to the next. However, as in any complex human undertaking, challenges occasionally crop up. In this chapter, we address both the routine matters involved in working through a meeting and the somewhat more complicated situations that might arise, and suggest ways of addressing each. (In Chapter 10, we consider in more depth some of the larger contextual challenges that affect groups, including lack of time to meet, school organization, and others.)

Here are some key responsibilities the facilitator has while a meeting is in progress:

- Cultivate "bi-focal vision."
- Help the group manage time.
- Help the group monitor its process and progress toward its goals.
- Help the group address more complex situations.

What we *don't* treat in detail in this chapter (or book) are ways in which a facilitator makes choices about and then implements specific tools, such as protocols, within teacher learning groups. Facilitators who make frequent use of protocols and other tools will find some of the moves we discuss here handy in those situations as well. For those less familiar with protocols, we offer a short introduction in Figure 5.1, Protocol Primer, and Figure 5.2 Some Protocols and Their Purposes. (Additional resources for using protocols, including *Looking Together at Student Work*, *The Facilitator's Book of Questions*, *The Power of Protocols*, and the School Reform Initiative website, are found in Appendix: Resources.)

Figure 5.1. Protocol Primer

In this book, we refer frequently to *protocols*. Many teachers will be familiar with the use of protocols for examining student work, providing feedback on one another's instruction, exploring professional dilemmas, and other purposes. For other educators, the term may be unfamiliar (at least in this context). Here, we offer some basic information about protocols.

What are protocols?

Protocols are structures that enable a group to engage in focused professional conversation. Many, though not all, protocols guide a group in looking carefully and collaboratively at student and teacher work in order to learn from it. Though different protocols vary in significant features, they all do two things:

- Provide a series of steps that a group follows (for example, presentation of a focusing problem, clarifying questions, review of student work samples, feedback to the presenter, and so on)
- Specify the roles different people in the group will play (typically, a facilitator, a presenter, and participants)

A protocol may take as little as 5 or 10 minutes to complete (for instance, the Microlab Protocol) or as long as an hour or more (for example, a full-blown Consultancy); most fall somewhere in between (20–45 minutes).

Things to keep in mind about protocols

- Protocols are not the same thing as a meeting agenda, although some protocols can take up a full meeting. A well-crafted agenda will include a sequence of activities that work together, one or more of which might be protocols.
- A protocol serves as a guide for the conversation, not a script. The facilitator and the group will always need to make decisions about how much time is appropriate for a given step, when to pause to reflect on the group's goals, and how to adapt the protocol—or even set it aside if it is not helping the group achieve its goal.

Figure 5.2. Some Protocols and Their Purposes

Protocol	Focus of the Protocol	Details about the Purpose
Protocols for EVALUATING (Identifying Strengths and Weaknesses) & IMPROVING CURRICULUM & INSTRUCTION		
Ladder of Feedback	Any specific plan, experience, or piece of work (a student assignment, a curriculum unit, a professional development experience).	The Ladder of Feedback and the Tuning Protocol are typical "problem-solving" protocols. In each of these protocols, participants examine particular pieces of student work or teacher/administrator work (curriculum plans, a draft of an agenda for a meeting, a proposal for a new project, and so on). Participants then evaluate the work (identifying strengths and weaknesses) and, finally, offer suggestions for improving it.
Tuning Protocol	Usually a specific assignment, accompanied by several samples of the student work that was done in response to the assignment, and possibly the rubric used for grading.	
Success Analysis Protocol	An assignment, unit, or learning experience that was especially successful (Actual assignment need not be used—the presenter's recollection of the assignment or experience will suffice).	The process of evaluation in this protocol usually involves identifying *only* strengths, not weaknesses. From the analysis of the strengths, generalizations are drawn that can lead to improving other lessons and curriculum units in the future.
Brainstorming Possibilities Protocol	Usually a specific and concrete problem that needs to be addressed or resolved. Usually the presenter gives a brief verbal description of the problem (samples of student and/or teacher work are usually not presented).	This protocol skips the process of evaluating altogether. The group simply accepts the presenter's description of the problem and moves straight to offering suggestions for improving or ameliorating it.

Protocol	Focus of the Protocol	Details about the Purpose
Protocols for DEVELOPING A DEEPER UNDERSTANDING OF STUDENT LEARNING & THINKING		
Collaborative Assessment Conference	Usually work from a single student (can be a single sample of work or multiple samples from the same student) carried out in response to a relatively open-ended assignment.	Both of these protocols are designed to engage participants in considering the student work from the student's perspective: What was the student learning or thinking as she carried out this work? What leads us to say so? Neither of these protocols asks the participants to engage in critique or problem solving. Instead, the protocols invite participants to focus on careful observation and question-raising. Both of these protocols guide participants to reflect deeply on their own practice, rather than to generate solutions or ideas for someone else.
Looking at Student Thinking Protocol (LAST)	Usually student work from an assignment designed to elicit students' thinking. (Can be a single sample of work from one student, or samples from several students done in response to the same assignment or prompt).	
Protocols for DEVELOPING A DEEPER UNDERSTANDING OF DILEMMAS OR PROBLEMS		
Consultancy Protocol	A dilemma faced by an individual or a group.	Though suggestions for addressing the dilemma may emerge in these protocols, their main focus is to lead both presenter and participants to a deeper understanding of the true nature of the dilemma, including the unspoken assumptions that underpin it.
Issaquah Protocol	A dilemma faced by an individual or a group.	
Protocols for GUIDING GROUP DISCUSSION OF A SHARED TEXT, EXPERIENCE, or ISSUE		
Microlab Protocol	Group discussion of a shared experience (such as a workshop), a text, or a specific set of questions (usually posed to the group by a facilitator).	This protocol allows each participant to share her thoughts about a text, experience, or specific question. This individual sharing is usually followed by a more general discussion, either in small groups or as a whole group.
Text-Based Seminar	Group discussion of a text that all participants have read.	In both of these protocols, participants discuss a text that all have read. (It is essential that all participants have copies of the text in front of them during the protocol.) The Text-Based Seminar depends more heavily on the guidance of a facilitator and can be shaped with specific questions that the facilitator offers the group for consideration. The Save the Last Word protocol gives participants more opportunity to shape the focus of the discussion.
Save the Last Word for Me	Group discussion of a text that all participants have read.	

Adapted from "A Guide to Using Protocols" by Gene Thompson-Grove, 2002, in *The School Reform Initiative Resource and Protocol Book 3.0* (www.schoolreforminitiative.org)

CULTIVATE "BI-FOCAL" VISION

The ability to focus simultaneously on content and process is an essential skill for facilitators of learning groups. Helping group members cultivate this kind of "bi-focal" vision is also important. An exclusive focus on the content of the discussion means that the group can lose sight of its overall goals and wander into interesting but nevertheless tangential discussions. And too much focus on process can lead to an overly rigid adherence to an agenda when a more flexible response to emerging issues or questions is needed. This bi-focal vision allows you to recognize and respond to moments in the meeting when the group's process and goals seem to be diverging.

POSSIBLE FACILITATION MOVES

Listen-Describe-Invite-Propose: A facilitation routine.

We suggest here a set of moves that, taken together, form a kind of "facilitation routine." This routine—like the thinking routines developed by Ron Ritchhart and colleagues (Ritchhart, Church, & Morrison, 2011)—is a short set of steps that can be used in almost any meeting situation in which you think intervention might be helpful. These steps, usually carried out in quick succession, look like this:

- *Listen.* Both listening and observing can be difficult if you're talking a lot. In general, good facilitators aim to listen and observe more than they talk.
- *Describe.* If you sense that something is not proceeding as planned or that the group's work is becoming less productive, find a moment to invite the group to pause for a "process check" and describe for the group what you are noticing. Be as specific and nonjudgmental as you can in your description—not simply "I think we're off topic" but "We had planned to talk about Y and now most of the comments I'm hearing are focused on Z."
- *Invite.* After sharing your observations, you can invite the group's thoughts: "Are others noticing the same thing? Are you seeing something else?" In some instances, you might want to follow up with one or two questions, for example: "Any thoughts on why topic Z seems more compelling than our originally planned agenda?" And, in preparation for the next step (proposing an action), you might invite thoughts on what to do next.

- *Propose.* In some situations, proposing a next step will be fairly easy because it will be obvious to everyone. For example, you notice and point out that the group is off topic, everyone agrees that they simply got caught up in a relatively unimportant digression, and the group returns to the original topic. In other situations, the next steps are not as clear. In such cases, you might try offering several options to the group. Another move is to gather the group's input about next steps before making a proposal. Remember, the facilitator's role is to help the group carry out its work—not to orchestrate its actions minute-to-minute. When you are unsure about how to proceed, consulting with the group is usually a good option; in addition to ensuring that the group is "on board" for the next steps, such consultation provides an opportunity for everyone in the group to cultivate bi-focal vision.

Invite collaborative decisionmaking whenever possible.

Another way to help the group develop its capacity to focus on both content and process is to facilitate collaborative decisionmaking when questions arise about the group's focus or next steps—for example, whether to revise the agenda mid-meeting. Such conversations help all group members stay mindful of the larger picture of the group's work (rather than merely the conversation of the moment). They also serve as a reminder that the facilitator supports the group in its work and learning rather than directly leading all aspects of the work.

Such collaborative decisionmaking can pose some challenges. Usually, the decision-making needs to happen quickly. There are ways to get a swift read on which way the group is leaning—asking for a show of hands, for example, or asking people to put thumbs up (to agree), thumbs down (to disagree), or thumbs sideways (to indicate that either they don't have a strong opinion or don't understand enough to cast a "yea" or "nay" vote). Ideally, the group's decisions will be based on consensus, but sometimes the will of the majority will have to do. If there is disagreement, the group often appreciates the efficiency of the facilitator making the call.

HELP THE GROUP MANAGE TIME

Teacher learning groups typically face two kinds of time-related challenges. The first is finding time for the group to hold its meetings. We discuss this challenge in Chapter 10. The focus of this section is the second time-related challenge: managing use of time *within* meetings in ways that help the group's work and learning progress.

The facilitator's responsibility for helping the group to use its time well begins even before the meeting, with planning a workable agenda (see Chapter 3). The time-managing responsibility continues in the beginning stage of the meeting as the facilitator reviews the agenda with the group and makes sure the group is clear about how time will be monitored during the meeting—whether that will be handled by a designated timekeeper or by the facilitator herself, perhaps using a device such as a kitchen timer or smartphone alarm (see Chapter 4).

Even with thoughtful preparation, managing time during a meeting can present challenges. The best agenda is only an educated guess about how the meeting will play out, even if it includes projected times for each activity (for instance, "discussion of new curriculum guides–15 minutes; debriefing peer observations–20 minutes"). In addition, learning to work as a group within specific time frames is an acquired skill. Even with a facilitator and a time-keeper, discussions can spill over beyond their agenda-established boundaries, especially when a group is just beginning its work.

POSSIBLE FACILITATION MOVES

Remind the group that the responsibility for using time well is a shared one.

The group may need a reminder during the meeting that all members share responsibility for ensuring that the group accomplishes what it needs to. (For some groups, this responsibility is named as one of its norms, making it easy for the group to review it.) For groups in the early stages of formation, especially, some members can slip into thinking that the facilitator "runs" the meeting and the timekeeper (if the group has designated one) is "in charge" of time. But teacher learning groups differ from most meetings people are used to attending. In a teacher learning group, the participants maintain collective responsibility for the direction and progress of the group's learning and work. Although it is important to have a facilitator and (perhaps) a designated timekeeper, such roles exist to help the group monitor itself, not to relieve the group of all responsibility for these functions. An occasional gentle reminder of this important difference may be helpful to the group as it works.

Help the group revise the agenda as the meeting progresses.

Agendas function as guides, with the times assigned to each activity serving as estimates, not rigid limits. The facilitator always balances those projected times with the group's and her own assessment of the content and nature of the group's activity at any given point—in terms of engagement, inclusiveness, and focus on the identified problem or question. If timekeeping is functioning well in a meeting, the group receives a signal—either from the facilitator, the timekeeper, or the digital alarm—2 to 5 minutes before the projected end of a segment. At this point, the group needs to make a decision: "Can we wrap up this activity in the next few minutes and make a transition to the next thing on the agenda? Or do we need more time?"

The group may decide that it needs more time than was originally designated for the activity. Of course, when adding time to one part of an agenda, another part will have to be shortened, or perhaps eliminated altogether. The facilitator can make a recommendation about this or can ask the group to give some brief thoughts: "Okay, we want to give this discussion 10 more minutes. That means we need to cut something else. Suggestions?" Sometimes it is possible to postpone an activity until a future meeting or to handle it outside of the meeting. The facilitator or the group's note-taker should keep track of the activities and discussions that the group postpones (sometimes making a visual "parking lot" on chart paper or whiteboard) so that they can be addressed at a later time.

Mark explicitly the transition from activity to activity.

Even when it's clear that a transition is needed, helping the group make that transition can still be challenging. Sometimes, the conversation at hand needs more attention—and yet, other pressing issues on the agenda can't be shortened or postponed. Sometimes, the facilitator can help the situation simply by acknowledging the difficulty: "Looks like we're not going to be able to resolve this challenge right now, given what else we have to accomplish. Let's spend a couple of minutes naming briefly the questions and issues that we'll have to leave unaddressed. We'll capture them in our notes, and then move on to the other urgent things we have to get to today."

Sometimes (very occasionally!), it happens that the flow of activities in a meeting goes exactly according to plan: Activities take the amount of time allotted on the agenda, and one flows smoothly into the next with no apparent need for facilitation. Though this is not the typical state of affairs for most learning group meetings, especially in the early stages, it's great when it happens. However, even in these meetings that seem to run themselves, it is still important for the facilitator to mark transitions, if for no other reason than to make sure they are made thoughtfully rather than simply expeditiously—for example: "Okay, from the last few comments, it sounds like we've made the transition to the next thing on the agenda. Let's just check to see if anyone else would like to add a comment to the previous topic before we completely shift gears."

HELP THE GROUP MONITOR PROCESS AND
PROGRESS TOWARD ITS GOALS

For any group, challenges can arise in how it carries out the agreed-upon processes or in how it focuses on the agreed-upon goals. Although these challenges can take many different forms, we have found they generally fall into three broad categories: "drift," "shift," and "rift."

"Drift"

Drift occurs when a group goes off on a tangent or detour, straying from either its established process or its stated goals. Some amount of drift in a meeting is to be expected; after all, group learning is a social process. Asides, jokes, anecdotes, and reminiscences—some of which may be related only minimally or not all to the focus of the conversation—are a normal and even productive part of the process. They allow the group to laugh together or to take a brief, collective "breather" in the middle of an intense discussion. Often, drift is just a momentary blip in the course of the conversation, and the group returns to its focus without any need for facilitator intervention. However, if an aside turns into several minutes of discussion unrelated to the group's process or goals, the facilitator should be prepared to help the group refocus.

POSSIBLE FACILITATION MOVES FOR ADDRESSING DRIFT

Listen-Describe-Invite-Propose.

In the case of drift, this whole facilitation routine, introduced earlier, might take less than a minute: "Can I do a quick process check? Feels like we've had a pretty good debriefing of last night's baseball game. . . . Is anyone else feeling like we've strayed a bit from the meeting focus? Perhaps we could turn back to the agenda now . . ."

For occasional drift: Use body language.

If the group has strayed off topic only briefly, it might be possible to help the group refocus without verbal intervention. Glancing at your watch, pulling your copy of the agenda toward you, or leaning forward to study it might be enough of a cue for the group to return to the topic.

*For more persistent drift: Invite more extended
reflection on process at the end of the meeting.*

As we describe in Chapter 6, an important part of wrapping up a meeting
is the opportunity for the group to reflect on both process and content. If
you find drift is a persistent or recurring problem for the group over several
meetings, you might try saving a few extra minutes at the end of one meeting
to share your observations and invite group members into a more extended
reflection on the issue. These reflections might be conducted first in writing
and then through discussion.

"Shift"

A *shift* is when the content of the discussion changes in a more significant way.
This occurs when the group, or a subset of the group, begins to engage with
another topic, one that may be related to the designated focus but is not always.
In this case, it feels like a new topic has nudged the old one aside. A similar kind
of shift might happen in terms of the group's process: Although the group has
agreed to use one process or protocol for its conversation, members of the group
find themselves consistently veering toward another kind of interaction. Unlike
drift, which can sometimes correct itself, a shift usually needs more direct facilitator intervention, both to call the group's attention to the (often inadvertent)
alteration in process or focus and to help the group to work out the best response: Should we continue with the new topic/process or return to the original?

POSSIBLE FACILITATION MOVES FOR ADDRESSING SHIFT

---

*Help the group identify an emergent goal or
question and adjust the agenda to support it.*

A shift from the originally articulated goal or question may signal that the
original plan wasn't quite right or that an important new goal has emerged.
If this seems to be the case, you might use the facilitation routine Listen-
Describe-Invite-Propose (introduced above) to open a brief discussion about
whether to return to the original plan or to reshape the meeting agenda to
accommodate the new goal or question. If the group opts for spending time
on the new issue, then usually the group (supported by the facilitator) also
needs to make some quick decisions about what else on the agenda needs to
be revised in order to accommodate the new focus. Whether the group decides

to pursue a new goal or stick with the old, documenting whatever has to be postponed is essential for future meetings.

For more persistent shifts: Encourage more focus.

It might be that your group shifts away from the agenda and into important new topics or processes every time it meets. A certain amount of this kind of shifting, especially in the early stages of a learning group, is to be expected: Developing a focus and formulating goals is often one of the most challenging tasks of a learning group. Figuring out which processes best support which kinds of discussion also takes some practice.

If, however, the shifting continues in meeting after meeting, the group may have succumbed to a common problem in learning groups: the tendency to move on to a new issue when progress on the original one seems slow. Given the complexity of the issues that teacher learning groups typically take on, the group needs to cultivate its capacity to dwell with challenges, to work in ambiguous problem spaces, and to resist the temptation toward quick fixes. If you notice the group shifting frequently, you might simply share that observation with the group and ask if they would be willing to try sticking with the originally planned focus the next time a new one emerges (while noting the new one, of course).

"Rift"

A third, somewhat thornier, situation occurs when one participant tries repeatedly to refocus the discussion on a question, problem, or topic of her own particular interest or when one participant pushes for a different process than the one the group has agreed upon. This kind of *rift* between one group member's preferred way of working and the rest of the group's efforts might arise intentionally: The person introducing the different topic or resisting the group's process does so consciously, in the belief that the topic or process she is suggesting would in fact be better for the whole group. Or it might arise unintentionally, with the "rifter" acting out of habit or from lack of awareness of the rest of the group's efforts. Either way, this is another situation that usually calls for direct facilitator intervention.

POSSIBLE FACILITATION MOVES FOR ADDRESSING RIFT

Clarify the goal and/or process for all participants.

When one person seems dedicated to a particular set of issues that clearly diverges from the central focus of the group, it's possible that that person has simply misunderstood the group's focus or agenda. As the facilitator, you can help by both allowing for the possibility of such a misunderstanding and taking on at least some of the responsibility for creating it: "Clara, may I interrupt? I think we might have a misunderstanding about what's happening in the meeting right now. I hear you sharing your ideas about which textbook we should be using for the 7th-graders, but as I understand it, our goal for the next 30 minutes is to examine these student work samples to identify our students' biggest challenges. I might not have made that clear in my overview of the agenda. Does that seem clearer to everyone now?"

Defer the off-topic issue to a later meeting.

If the topic being raised by a single person is one that seems relevant to the group's work despite not being the immediate focus, you might suggest that it be put on hold: "Clara, it seems like the choice of textbook is really important to you. I think most of us would agree with you that it is an important issue. Because we can only focus as a group on one thing at a time, could we put that issue in the 'parking lot' for now so that we can come back to it at a time when we can give it the attention it needs?"

Talk with the participant outside of the meeting.

Sometimes, despite gentle reminders and deflections, a participant won't be put off her preferred topic. The situation might require a more extended conversation outside of the meeting that will enable you and the participant to talk in more depth about her topic and how it relates—or doesn't—to the focus of the group, and whether there might be other ways for her to explore that issue either within or independently of the group.

HELP THE GROUP ADDRESS MORE COMPLEX SITUATIONS

Being a member of a teacher learning group is hard work—*rewarding* hard work, but hard work nevertheless. The focus of most teacher learning groups is how to better support student learning—a topic that is both profoundly important and also bafflingly complex. When the stakes are high and the problem space is ambiguous, the work is likely to involve some serious bumps. At least occasionally, dead ends will be encountered, knotty problems will remain stubbornly knotted, and frustrations will surface.

In some ways, when these things happen, it will be a good sign: It means the group is digging deeply enough to get to the hard questions—the pursuit of which can lead to new and more robust understandings about how to help students learn. At least you'll know that you have avoided the pitfall that traps many teacher learning groups, the "culture of nice" (MacDonald, 2011)—that is, the impulse to keep conversation so cordial and problem-free that the group never even broaches the really difficult—and really important—topics. Getting beyond this overly cordial culture involves sharing different perspectives, even questioning one another's interpretations (respectfully, of course).

So, there is a real possibility that, at some point, your group will run into a difficult situation. No guide could enumerate all the various challenges your group might encounter. However, we can share with you a few useful (and often underused) moves for your facilitator repertoire.

POSSIBLE FACILITATION MOVES FOR ADDRESSING MORE COMPLEX SITUATIONS

Call for a minute or two of quiet.

This move is useful for helping to reorient the group in almost any situation, whether tensions are high are not—but especially when tensions are high. Simply say to the group: "It looks to me like we have reached a challenging place here. We've got serious differences of opinion about how we should handle X, and it's not immediately clear to me how to proceed. Can we take just a couple of minutes of quiet, to give us all a chance to reflect on where to go from here? Then we can talk about possibilities." Even if, in those 2 minutes, you don't see an obvious next step, you will be in a better (more settled, more reflective) mindset for facilitating the next part of the conversation as the group figures out what to do.

Ask questions in order to understand differences of opinion.

Sometimes, conflicts or disagreements arise in a group, and you might feel yourself tempted to think that someone in the group—particularly someone whose ideas or opinions are very different from yours—is simply being unreasonable. When this feeling hits, consider it a call to a closer study of the situation. The truth is that people, by and large, behave in ways that make sense to them—people rarely come up with random objections simply for the sake of being difficult.

The question to ask is: What is the other person seeing that makes her objections or concerns seem (at least to her) not only reasonable but pressing? In other words, what does the world look like from where she sits? Clarifying questions often help—for example, "When you say that it's important for the whole grade level to have a standardized assessment, can you describe a bit more about what you're thinking of when you say 'assessment'?" Sometimes more probing questions are needed—for example: "As you see it, how do standardized assessments support student learning?" or "What's your biggest concern if we don't put standardized assessments in place for the whole grade level?"

Turn group members' questions back to the group.

One frequent concern of new facilitators is how to handle the challenging questions posed by group members who don't like or don't agree with certain aspects of the group's work: "I don't know why we're even thinking about this issue anyway—the district office is just going to tell us what to do in the end." "Why do we have to use this protocol—why can't we just talk?" In Chapter 4, we consider how norm setting can help address some of these issues. But even with careful groundwork laid, there can still be occasions when group members have concerns about the group's direction.

One way to handle such questions is not to answer them but instead, at the appropriate moment, to open them up to the group for responses. You may want to address such questions as they come up, or you might want to ask if the participant would be okay with waiting until the debriefing portion of the meeting to discuss it. Some possible language: "Good question, Amanda—it can be useful to revisit our goals [and/or processes] periodically and make sure they help us focus on what's most important. Let's check in with the group about that: How has the experience of using this protocol been for you?" Or "Do others feel like our focus question is off the mark?" Almost always, some diversity of opinion will emerge in response to this move: Some will share the concern; others will voice their appreciation for the group's goals and processes. Your role, at this point, is usually not to defend the group's process but to listen carefully and to acknowledge the diversity of reactions, pointing out to the group that such differences are a normal part of group learning— challenging to manage, perhaps, but also enriching for the discussion. Some suggestions for improving the group's process or goals may emerge from this conversation—if so, great. If concerns linger, you might offer to talk with people outside of the group or plan for a longer conversation at the next meeting.

Choose a good protocol.

When a group is having difficulty communicating, an appropriate protocol can go a long way toward helping participants hear and respond to one another. If you're not familiar with a variety of protocols, it's worth spending some time to familiarize yourself with a few of those intended to help a group to have challenging conversations—for instance, the Consultancy for unpacking a dilemma, or the Ladder of Feedback for analyzing and improving a particular project, situation, or set of practices. (The Ladder of Feedback is included in Chapter 10; for more information on protocols, see Chapter 5, Figures 5.1, Protocol Primer, and 5.2, Some Protocols and Their Purposes, and Appendix: Resources.)

Assume good intent.

Different people have different ideas about what constitutes appropriate participation in groups and discussions. Not every joke, comment, or expression of body language that at first may seem to be aimed at derailing the group's process is actually meant to. Assume good intent for as long as possible, allowing for the possibility that everyone in the room is there for a legitimate reason and is participating to the best of her ability. Even if a group member makes it clear that she is disgruntled with something in the group's work, accepting comments or questions in a better spirit than perhaps they were offered can help nudge the participant into a more open frame of mind.

CHAPTER 6

Closing the Meeting

Bringing a teacher learning group meeting to a close almost always presents something of a puzzle: It is not always clear what constitutes a productive and satisfying conclusion to this kind of meeting. Probably, most people could recount one or two unsatisfying or unproductive conclusions: Time runs out in the middle of a complex discussion; group members jump up, collect their things, and head for the door—despite the fact that a few people are attempting to carry on the trailing threads of the conversation—while the person leading the meeting yells out barely audible announcements over the sound of the ringing school bell. Definitely unsatisfying. Definitely not productive.

But the better ending to the meeting—the ending that feels good, moves the work ahead, and supports learning—is not entirely straightforward. On the one hand, there is a certain satisfaction to ending a meeting with an "Aha!" moment—a sudden insight into a knotty problem or question. It's also great when specific tasks get accomplished by the meeting's end and the whole group can dust off their hands in a satisfied manner and give a congratulatory head nod.

The problem is that the groups we're talking about here are teacher *learning* groups, and learning—especially learning about issues as complex as teaching and learning in pre-K–12 classrooms—usually doesn't lend itself to neat and timely endings. Often, the meeting ends with more questions on the table than there were at the beginning of the meeting. The group comes to the end of the conversation and is not absolutely certain about what the best next steps might be. Matters seem more complex rather than less.

So bringing a teacher learning group meeting to a conclusion involves a balance: on the one hand, allowing the group a thoughtful and coherent conclusion to this particular episode in its collective learning; on the other, not forcing artificially neat conclusions about what has been learned or accomplished. The facilitator undertakes key responsibilities in the process of closing the meeting in order to help the group both maintain this balance and set the stage for ongoing learning in between meetings and in meetings to come. Those responsibilities include:

- Invite the group to express appreciation.
- Help the group reflect on the content of the meeting.

- Help the group reflect on the process of the meeting.
- Help the group identify next steps.
- Gather documentation artifacts from the meeting.
- Restore the space (if necessary).

It may seem impossible to do everything we detail below in the last 5 to 10 minutes of a meeting—which is typically as much time as can be devoted to the conclusion of a meeting, given the scant 40–50 minutes that most groups have available. It might help to keep two things in mind: First, no meeting addresses all these points equally well. One week, the group's reflection on content might take precedence; another week, the group might spend more time on process reflections and gathering and organizing documentation. Second, as the group works together over time and develops its routines, it will become easier to accomplish more in less time.

INVITE THE GROUP TO EXPRESS APPRECIATION

Fulfilling this responsibility takes little time but sends a powerful message to the group: The collective learning depends upon individuals within the group stepping up at different times and in different ways to support the whole group's learning.

POSSIBLE FACILITATION MOVES

Call out and applaud the participants who played particular roles.

For group members who played particular roles in the meeting, the facilitator might simply take a moment to call out their names and mention what they did to contribute: "Let's take a minute to recognize Rachel for bringing a question about her teaching along with samples of student work from her classroom. Sharing her work enabled all of us to learn about the issue" or "And let's not forget to thank Carlos for letting us use his classroom today. We promise to put the desks back before we go!" (Time: 1–2 minutes)

"I reinforce . . ."

This approach to expressing appreciation, borrowed from the theater world, takes a bit longer but gives everyone in the group a chance to call out and acknowledge the contribution of someone else in the group. One person in the group begins by saying, "I reinforce . . ." and completes the sentence by naming something that someone in the group said or did that was helpful. For example: "I want to reinforce the point Nick made during our discussion about the importance of slowing down to really look at our students' work rather than rushing through it when we're grading." "I reinforce the importance of having snacks—thanks for bringing them, Sara!" The group continues around the circle until everyone has had a chance to express appreciation for someone else's contribution to the work. (Time: 3–5 minutes)

"Give ourselves a hand!"

Take a moment to recognize the good work of the group as a whole, in terms of commitment, accomplishment, and openness to new questions and challenges. (Time: 1 minute)

HELP THE GROUP REFLECT ON THE CONTENT OF THE MEETING

This responsibility involves asking participants to reflect on what they have learned about the question or problem the group was addressing and/or the task it was working on. Although reflection on content is usually done jointly with reflection on process, we treat them separately here because it is important to differentiate between the learning and the process that supports that learning.

Learning sometimes takes the form of clear-cut realizations or "aha's" that occur within meetings. And it is gratifying when one can extract such crystallizations of learning from a meeting. Just because it is not always (or even regularly) possible to do so does not mean that learning is not going on. It is the facilitator's job to help the group bring to the surface learning in the varied forms it takes, including new perspectives, greater understanding, hypotheses, questions, and puzzles. In fact, it is often the questions and puzzles that will be most stimulating of future learning—as long as they are named and documented (as we discuss below).

POSSIBLE FACILITATION MOVES

Monitor time carefully.

Perhaps the most important move here is one that happens even before the end of the meeting: keeping an eye on time to ensure that the group can spend at least 5 minutes on reflection before the meeting ends—no mean trick, but definitely do-able, especially if you have invited another group member to help with timekeeping (see Chapter 4). You might begin by saying, "Let's take a few minutes now to reflect on our learning in the meeting, especially in relation to our goal or focus [recap goal/focus briefly]." You can then use one or more of the moves listed here to help participants describe and document their ideas, insights, questions, and puzzles.

Invite group members to complete a reflection sheet.

Prepare a reflection sheet (Figure 6.1 provides one example) that asks participants to reflect on both what they learned and how the group's process supported the learning. If there's time, group members can share one highlight from their written responses out loud in the group. If time is short, either the documenter or the facilitator can compile the written responses after the meeting and email them out to the group. (Time: 3–8 minutes, depending on group size and whether highlights are shared out loud in the group)

Do a closing "whip."

Invite the group to reflect silently (perhaps for 20–30 seconds) about the most important insight or puzzle they are taking away from conversation. Encourage participants to formulate their insight or puzzle in a phrase or short sentence. Then, going in order around the circle, each person shares their phrase or short sentence, with no commentary or questions from others. Participants who aren't ready—or would prefer not to share—can say "pass" when their turn comes. (Because participants don't usually write anything prior to their sharing, request that someone take notes to help document these short reflections.) (Time: 1–4 minutes, depending on group size)

Figure 6.1. Sample Reflection Sheet

One thing I learned in today's meeting:

One question I leave the meeting with:

One suggestion for the next meeting or future meetings—either content or process:

Other comments about content or process:

Invite summary statements from the group.

Ask if anyone in the group would like to offer a brief summary of the group's learning, and then invite other perspectives that clarify or expand on the statement. Another move for distilling key ideas is the "Headlines" exercise developed by Ron Ritchhart and colleagues (see Figure 6.2) in which participants (either individually or in pairs) develop a headline that captures a central idea or question that the group focused on that day. (Time: 3–5 minutes)

Figure 6.2. Headlines Routine

- Think of the big ideas and important themes in what you have been learning.
- Write a headline for this topic or issue that captures the essence of an idea or question that you feel is significant.

(Note: Headlines are normally a phrase or sentence at most.)

Adapted from Ron Ritchhart, Mark Church, and Karen Morrison, *Making Thinking Visible: How to Promote Engagement, Understanding, and Independence for All Learners*, 2011.

Whatever form the reflection takes, the facilitator (or the group members helping to document the meeting) should collect or record the reflections. These are crucial artifacts for tracking the group's learning and planning future meetings.

HELP THE GROUP REFLECT ON THE PROCESS OF THE MEETING

Reflection on process (sometimes called "debriefing the meeting") can be an easy step to skip. Having reflected on the content of the meeting, group members might feel as though the "important" reflection is done: If there's time for a debriefing of the process, fine; if not—well, there's always next time. The problem with this approach to "process reflection" is that a group can sometimes go weeks or even months without ever considering some of the most critical questions to ensuring the group's success: Are we using our time well? Are the tools (protocols and activities) we're using and the way we structure the meetings helping us get where we need to go? How can we work together more effectively?

Through thoughtful and deliberate reflection on the process, the group learns to collaborate more skillfully, enabling the group as a whole as well as individual members to accomplish (and learn) more. Such reflection also helps the facilitator learn how to support the group's learning even more effectively—and how to develop her own facilitation practice.

POSSIBLE FACILITATION MOVES

Any of the moves described in the section on reflection on content can also be used for—and combined with—reflecting on process. In addition, you might consider the following moves.

Hand off facilitation duties to the backup ("pinch-hit") facilitator.

Because the facilitator's work is often a key part of what participants discuss when they reflect on process, you might want to ask someone else in the group to facilitate this part of the meeting. This allows you to concentrate on the substance of what group members share without having the burden of managing the process. It also avoids the potential awkwardness of group members having to name concerns about your (the facilitator's) work directly to you.

Take regular, informal surveys of the group members.

After reflecting on content, you might say: "Let's spend a couple more minutes talking about our process: What worked? What might we change or try differently in our next meeting?" Participants might simply respond verbally to these prompts, perhaps after a brief pause for reflection. (Time: 3–5 minutes)

Occasionally invite more in-depth reflection on process.

Given limited time, it's likely that the regular reflections on process will be quick. If the group is meeting over an extended period of time (say, a semester or a year), take one or two meetings to have a more extended discussion of the group's process—what's working, what's problematic, and how to improve. This reflection should also include a review of the group's norms. You might try using the Ladder of Feedback protocol to guide this conversation (see Figure 10.1 in Chapter 10). (Time: 15–30 minutes)

Whatever form the process reflections take, the facilitator (or another person in the group serving as documenter) should record or collect the reflections for documentation and planning purposes.

HELP THE GROUP IDENTIFY NEXT STEPS FOR ITS LEARNING AND WORK

One of the most common complaints about teacher groups is that the meetings "don't go anywhere." Even when the discussion in a meeting is collegial in spirit and rich in ideas, there is often little or no clear direction for the group's next steps. This can lead participants to "check out" (physically or mentally) from the group's meetings.

Groups focused primarily on completing a task may find it easy to articulate next steps. For groups focused on learning, getting clear about next steps may be a bit trickier but no less important. In fact, one of the primary purposes for reflecting on content and process is to help the group determine collaboratively some of the implications for its ongoing work. Without facilitation, though, this is unlikely to happen on its own.

POSSIBLE FACILITATION MOVES

Brainstorm ideas for next meeting.

Based on the group's reflections on content, the facilitator might ask the group for ideas about how to use the next meeting. This might include identifying one or more of the participants to play a role in the meeting (for example, presenting a problem of practice, sharing samples of student work, or leading a discussion on a particular topic). It is not always possible or even advisable to create the agenda for the next meeting at the end of the current one. The facilitator might simply collect ideas to use in drafting an agenda that can be shared with the group for feedback in between meetings, either in person or online. (See Chapter 3.) (Time: 3–6 minutes)

Encourage depth.

The facilitator can be especially useful in helping the group resist the tendency to move on to something new rather than continuing the exploration of a problem or question. Of course, there are times when the group should move on, but often the most productive next step for a group's learning is to go deeper with a problem or question—bringing other relevant artifacts or data to examine, using a different activity or protocol, or focusing on a different set of students. (Time: 3–10 minutes, depending on the form discussion takes)

Decide how to share information with group members who were absent.

One easily overlooked aspect of concluding the meeting is to decide how key points from the meeting will be communicated to any group member who wasn't present. This could be done by the facilitator or by a teacher who will be in contact with the absent member. (Time: 1–3 minutes)

GATHER DOCUMENTATION ARTIFACTS FROM THE MEETING

In Chapter 4, we described documenting as one of the functions that support a group's learning. We also talked about the importance of the documenting function being shared among group members. It is especially important that the facilitator not spend all of her time taking notes. If the facilitator is busy trying to record everything that is said in the group, she will be less able to make the moves that are likely to support the group's learning during the meeting. At the same time, documenting the learning that goes on in a group is a crucial contribution to the group's learning. Fortunately, when it comes to documenting the group's learning, there are some relatively straightforward and easy moves the facilitator—or any group member—can make.

POSSIBLE FACILITATION MOVES

Gather artifacts from the meeting.

The facilitator (or a designated participant) can collect the artifacts used in the meeting, as well as any products created during the meeting. Artifacts might include any of the following (and many more):

- agenda
- handouts
- samples of teachers' curriculum or students' work.

Products created at the meeting might include:

- lists
- charts
- calendars
- written reflections or feedback sheets.

Note: Sometimes taking a photo on a cellphone or tablet is the quickest and easiest way to capture something—for example, when it is written on chart paper or a whiteboard. (Time: Ongoing during meeting plus 2–3 minutes at meeting's end)

Put artifacts into the appropriate file.

A simple filing system (perhaps one in which each meeting has its own folder) is probably best, but use whatever system is going to make documentation easiest for you and the group to retrieve and review it regularly. Remember that memory is fallible: Make sure you include pertinent information on every artifact you put in the folders: names, dates, grade level, and so forth.

As we note in Chapter 7, an effective way to build continuity and momentum in a series of meetings is to share some themes, questions, ideas, and so on from the reflections done in the previous meeting, especially if these relate to the goal for the meeting. Having the relevant file with you will allow you to do this in a quick and reliable way.

As more artifacts are stored and shared digitally, on a server or cloud, make sure electronic copies of meeting artifacts are stored in folders labeled with the dates of meetings. (Time: 1–2 minutes at the end of the meeting; time in between meetings to make sure files are up to date)

RESTORE THE SPACE (IF NECESSARY)

The point of this particular move is probably obvious . . .

POSSIBLE FACILITATION MOVE

Ask for help.

As with the setup of the room, you can ask the group to make sure the room is returned to the pre-meeting configuration. This won't take long, and teachers are used to doing this.

CHAPTER 7

Following Up on the Meeting

Thoughtful use of the time between meetings can serve to deepen the learning that happens in meetings. The follow-up work becomes especially important if the group's meetings are relatively brief and spaced more than a week apart. The facilitator might take on (or, in some cases, support others in taking on) one or more of the following responsibilities in the days following a meeting:

- Continue to gather documentation artifacts.
- Review documentation artifacts.
- Check in informally with participants.

Before you tackle any of these, you might find it helpful to make a conscious decision about how much time you are able to devote to follow-up activities. The challenge here is that there are so many good and useful ways to engage in follow-up work after a meeting is over—checking in individually with group members, writing up your notes, reviewing group members' written reflections, compiling and reviewing documentation, and so on. A facilitator trying conscientiously to address all possible aspects of follow-up work could easily feel overwhelmed . . . and then exhausted . . . and, ultimately, burned out—a state of affairs that serves no one.

The truth is that you do not need to engage in every type of follow-up activity after every meeting. Make choices: What will serve your group best? What do you have time for? If your group meets once a week, you might feel that you can give 30 minutes to follow up—perhaps 15 minutes to review the group's end-of-meeting reflections and 15 minutes to check in with one participant in person. If your group meets once every 2 weeks, you might be able to dedicate an hour to follow-up and reflection during the intervening 2-week stretch. The key here is to select, prioritize, and then rotate your choices over time. If you concentrated on in-person check-ins after the last meeting, you might focus more on the formal documentation of the group's work after the next one.

CONTINUE TO GATHER
DOCUMENTATION ARTIFACTS

If you asked group members to write out reflections that they didn't have time to share during the meeting, these need to be read and (ideally) shared with other group members (either electronically, if they can be easily scanned or transcribed, or in hard copy if they can't). If someone either recorded notes for the meeting or completed some other form of documentation that requires more processing, that documentation needs to be collected and put in either hard-copy or electronic folders (preferably both).

REVIEW DOCUMENTATION
ARTIFACTS

If the gathering phase of the documentation process has gone well, then at this point, you probably have a well-filled folder (on your desk or on your computer or server) containing a copy of the meeting agenda, copies of any protocols or activities the group used in the meeting, copies of student work or other artifacts that were shared, meeting notes (preferably written up by a group member other than you), perhaps some participants' written reflections about their learning, and maybe some notes that you jotted down during the meeting or afterward. If your group has met more than once, you might have several such well-filled folders that capture what the group has done and how group members see their learning developing. However, all of this documentation is more or less useless unless you and other group members *make time to review and reflect on it.*

POSSIBLE FACILITATION MOVES

Use available forms of documentation.

Notes and other records can help identify key questions and ideas that emerge within the meeting. These questions and ideas are crucial data for planning the next meeting. By documenting the group's work consistently and then looking for ways to integrate new ideas and questions into the ongoing work, the facilitator and the group create the conditions for learning to develop and deepen over time.

Use your judgment.

Some new ideas or questions might relate to existing group goals and can be consolidated or integrated with plans for an upcoming meeting. For example, reviewing test data may work well with a group's prior goal of identifying benchmarks for student work on specific tasks. Other emerging issues may be interesting but diverge from the established goals. As they review documentation, facilitators need to use their knowledge of the group's established goals, as well as their understanding of participants' priorities, to help the group make effective decisions about which ideas to take up in subsequent meetings.

Recognize constraints.

Of course, it isn't possible for any group to fully explore every idea or question that surfaces during a meeting. When it does not seem possible to incorporate an idea or question into an upcoming meeting, let group members know—privately to the person who brought it up and publicly within the group's meeting. For example, "Jessica made a really interesting suggestion about reviewing our IEP [Individualize Educational Program] process. This is probably going to take more time than we have in one or even a couple meetings, especially since we have committed to analyzing lesson plans for types of questions. Can we agree to consider this as a question or activity for next semester?"

Get other perspectives.

Once again, the facilitator is not alone in weighing "competing" demands on a group's meeting time. One of the purposes for checking in with participants (discussed below) is to get other perspectives on how the agenda for the group's next meeting(s) can best serve the group's goals and interests—and to encourage "ownership" of the group's process and content.

CHECK IN INFORMALLY
WITH PARTICIPANTS

Facilitators often find it helpful to talk informally with participants between meetings. They do this in order to:

- Get input on the agenda for the upcoming meeting/future meetings.
- Help a group member prepare for the upcoming meeting.
- Gain perspective on something a participant said or did in the meeting.
- Encourage a member to participate more (or more positively).

- Get feedback on the group's process.
- Get feedback on their facilitation.

Facilitators may check in with participants for other reasons, too. In doing these check-ins, the facilitator needs to be strategic and efficient. The moves below may help.

POSSIBLE FACILITATION MOVES

Prioritize.

It probably isn't possible to check in with everybody individually after every meeting. Try to get to the person or persons who may need support most and those who can contribute most to the upcoming meeting. For instance, you might have time only to check in with a teacher who seemed dissatisfied or confused about something that happened in the last meeting, another who will present a dilemma for the group to discuss at the next meeting, and a third who can give input on the agenda as you develop it. (If you only have time to get to one, pick the one who is likely to have the biggest impact on the group's next meeting.)

Distribute yourself.

Over the course of a month or so, try to check in with everybody in the group—even if there is no pressing reason to do so. Give all the participants in the group a chance to share how they think things are going, what they are learning from the group's meetings, and what they might like to do more of in the meetings.

Use technology.

It's great when you can speak to people face-to-face. But often the reality of teachers' lives makes it difficult to get the 5 or 10 minutes you need with a particular teacher within the time frame that you need it. Figure out the best way to communicate with individuals in the group between meetings. For some, this might be email, and for others instant messaging. In some cases, a Google Group or similar tool might be useful in supporting online discussions. These may or may not be the same communication tools you use when communicating with the whole group and other stakeholders (see below).

Differentiate.

Determine which check-in conversations should be one-on-one and which should be with the whole group. For example, you might use an email to the whole group or a message in Google Groups to ask for a volunteer to take notes at the next meeting or to solicit feedback on which of several possible activities seems most useful for the group's learning. On the other hand, a one-on-one (and face-to-face) dialogue might be more appropriate if, for example, you are asking about why a teacher responded to a colleague's question in a certain way or asking for feedback on your facilitation within the last meeting.

Make it a two-way street.

It's likely that, as the facilitator, you will be the one checking in with other participants in the group. However, it is very helpful to the facilitator, and healthy for the group, for participants to reach out to the facilitator between meetings with comments, questions, or requests. Invite participants to do so, let them know the best way to reach you, and respond promptly when they do—they'll be more likely to do it again.

These and other check-in moves give powerful signals to group members that their involvement is critical to the group's learning. They also provide opportunities for you as the facilitator to learn more about the individuals in the group, which will inform your facilitation.

COMMUNICATE FORMALLY WITH PARTICIPANTS AND OTHER STAKEHOLDERS

Communicating in more formal ways about the group's work with group members serves a number of key purposes, including these:

- Encouraging reflection on learning in between meetings.
- Encouraging preparation for upcoming meetings, both logistical (time, materials, and so on) and mental (getting into a frame of mind for collaborative learning).
- Creating artifacts that document the group's learning (to supplement those collected at the meeting).

Of course, the members of the group are the key "stakeholders" in the learning that goes on within the group, and so typically they are the main audience for any formal, post-meeting communication in which the facilitator summarizes or raises questions about the group's learning. However, a group's work is always part of the larger professional culture of the school. Others who have a stake (or a legitimate interest) in the group's work include administrators, coaches, staff developers, and even other facilitators and other groups. Communicating with these stakeholders serves to:

- Strengthen connections with other forms of professional learning in the school.
- Build support for the group's work.

POSSIBLE FACILITATION MOVES

Recap.

Send an email (and/or hard copy) to group members with a summary of key points discussed at the previous meeting, any decisions made, and a preview of the upcoming meeting. Invite group members to share comments, questions, and ideas online or with you individually.

Reach out.

Update administrators and other stakeholders. In many cases, the same communiqué that goes to the group can go to administrators and other stakeholders as well. A facilitator might also decide that a different or condensed version is more appropriate for non-group members. Remember that anything that goes out to a group member might be seen by others outside of the group. For this reason, don't include anything in the notes that you would not want to be seen by somebody outside the group.

Remind.

A day or two before an upcoming meeting, send a reminder to the group members (and, if appropriate, other stakeholders) along with the proposed agenda. Invite additional input from the group.

PART III

OPPORTUNITIES AND CHALLENGES

CHAPTER 8

Managing Productive Group Interactions

Like professionals everywhere, teachers want their meetings to be interesting, collegial, productive, and generative of learning. Most of the time, teachers participate in ways that contribute to meetings with these qualities. And yet, meetings do not always feel as collegial, productive, or learning-oriented as the facilitator and other group members would like.

Of course, the meeting's goals and the structures employed to achieve them (protocols, activities, and others) will influence a meeting's "feel," as well as how productive it is in terms of learning and getting things done. So will the interactions among participants. By and large, these interactions are positive and productive, but in some groups—at least at some points—they are not. Instead, they may feel frustrating, inequitable, even alienating.

A number of factors contribute to this state of affairs. In the sections that follow, we discuss three of the most common:

- Differences in individuals' points of view
- Differences in how individuals engage in meetings
- Differences in how individuals experience the group's autonomy

For each factor, we describe some ways it might affect group interactions. We also propose some possible facilitation moves for addressing these challenges.

DIFFERENCES IN INDIVIDUALS' POINTS OF VIEW

Groups are powerful vehicles for learning because individual members bring different experiences and points of view. When the group members engage these differences productively, the work is likely to be generative, interesting, and even personally satisfying. Meetings become opportunities to share experiences and perspectives, learn about others, make connections, and explore differences.

Often, difficulties occur not because there are different perspectives expressed within a discussion but because group members are uncomfortable with the idea of different points of view. This kind of discomfort can also develop when one person's perspective is presented as—or perceived as—critical or dismissive of another's. Differences of perspective on a question or issue related to teaching and learning will be shaped by many factors, including individuals' varied experiences and areas of expertise.

Differences in *experience* can take many forms—for example, experiences teaching at different grade levels ("I've taught it all, from preschool to high school . . .") or even in different countries ("When I taught in the Netherlands . . ."). But the most common difference is the number of years an individual has taught, whether she is an experienced teacher or a novice. In many groups, an (unspoken) norm exists: The perspectives of more experienced members are more valued than those of less experienced members. Though it is true that teachers (and all professionals) early in their career benefit from observing and listening to more experienced colleagues, their learning and the group's will be shortchanged if less experienced members are not invited to participate.

Consider, for example, a middle school team that includes teachers with 10 years or more of experience and one first-year teacher. In discussing how to support struggling readers, the new teacher is likely to have much less experience working with such students. However, in her teacher education program or student teaching, she may have learned a promising strategy for doing so that might be valuable for more experienced colleagues to learn about. Or she may have a question that opens up a valuable discussion for the whole group. However, she will be less likely to offer these if a senior colleague prefaces her remarks with a comment like, "When you've been doing this as long as I have, you'll see what I mean. . . ."

Similar challenges to group and individual learning emerge when one or more members of the group assume a privileged position in terms of *expertise* (for example, "I have been a trainer for the writing workshop approach . . ."). It is possible to share such expertise in ways that enhance the learning of the group. However, it becomes a problem if sharing expertise serves, intentionally or not, to devalue another member's perspective. In these less productive instances, some group members may be discouraged from making a contribution to the discussion (perhaps thinking to themselves, "Next time, I'll just keep it to myself").

Finally, individuals have their own convictions about issues of teaching and learning—for example, what should be taught or how something should be taught. These strongly held opinions are sometimes shaped by experience or expertise, but not always. They may come from a "gut feeling" or may relate to beliefs in other areas of a person's life: family, culture, faith, or politics. These differences in individual beliefs may emerge and complicate a group's interaction.

Some groups struggle, especially at first, with how to respond to differences in opinions when they surface. Some group members simply ignore differences when they come up, nodding politely and moving on. For other group members, differences of opinion might provoke defensive reactions, leading to situations in which one group member dismisses another's point of view as lacking value. In contrast to these approaches, acknowledging differences of opinion can result in all parties developing a greater understanding of and a broader perspective on the topic at hand.

POSSIBLE FACILITATION MOVES

Establish norms that explicitly encourage airing differing points of view.

Many groups adopt a norm that states, "There is no monopoly on expertise." This norm recognizes that a group member with years of teaching experience or a recognized area of expertise has a legitimate and useful perspective to share. But so does a brand-new teacher who has limited teaching experience— or someone who has never taught the subject being discussed but has a question or observation to make about it.

Establish norms that explicitly encourage productive responses to different points of view.

It is common among theater improvisers (and theater artists generally) to hear the expression "*Yes, and . . .*" This is shorthand for the quality actors strive for in how they respond to one another in creating and performing works for the stage. Rather than dismiss or reject (or try to top) a fellow actor's contribution, or "offer" (whether that offer consists of spoken words or a physical gesture), the goal is to accept it on its own terms and in some way build upon it. Doing so does not mean automatic or unquestioned agreement with the offer, but rather a deliberate attempt to take it seriously. A "Yes, and . . ." response in a teacher group might be to ask a clarifying question about a colleague's comment, take up an idea shared by another group member and build upon it, or suggest an alternative way to think about a question or issue.

When group members are avoiding differences,
name them yourself and invite conversation.

This is a version of the Listen-Describe-Invite-Propose facilitation routine outlined in Chapter 5. You might start off by saying, "Alysha, what you said is really interesting—it also sounds different to me from what Ryan just said about the same issue. Does it sound different to you, too? What do the two of you (or anyone else in the group) make of that difference?"

Encourage group members to respond directly to one another.

When group members are shying away from engaging one another's ideas directly, you might consider using a specific exercise to help them engage in more depth: Invite each person to contribute to the conversation, but only if she can begin her contribution by creating a direct connection to the comment that came before—either by building on that comment or by pointing out a contrast between that comment and what she would like to say. (Note: This should be understood as an exercise, not a rule for all discussions.)

DIFFERENCES IN HOW INDIVIDUALS ENGAGE IN MEETINGS

There is no shortage of lists of personality types you will find in meetings. For example, consider this one from the *CBS MoneyWatch* blog post entitled "5 Personalities That Wreck a Meeting." The post describes "the bully," "the non sequitur," "the would-be visionary," "the constant questioner," and "the rambler" (Vanderkam, 2012). Like many other taxonomies, this list dwells on the negative aspects of individual personalities (and how to counteract them). In reality, it is the differences in how individuals interact with others in the group that make meetings interesting and productive.

In some groups, differences in how individuals enter into and sustain a conversation seem to dovetail naturally to create a rich learning environment. "We just click," a participant in such a group might remark. But what if a group doesn't just click? What if participants' preferred ways of interacting make it more difficult for the group to work and learn together productively?

There is infinite variety in how individuals engage with one another within meetings. For example, one teacher might enter into discussions in a forceful, confident manner: "We should just do . . ." or (to another participant) "You should just do. . . ." If other members of the group find this off-putting or intimidating, they are likely to withdraw from the group's activity. By the same token, a member who consistently raises questions about the group's goals and process might be appreciated for reminding the group to reflect, or she might be perceived by some as slowing things down—or even as an annoying presence, best ignored. A colleague's silence might be recognized as thoughtful reflection, or an unspoken critique of the group's work.

Group members sometimes struggle with the balance between comfort and challenge. Some group members equate "respect" with giving others in the group a kind of blanket and unquestioning approval in everything they say and do. Concerned about being perceived as being judgmental, these participants err on the side of "the culture of nice" (MacDonald, 2011). But group members can err in the other direction, too, giving their unvarnished opinions on everything, regardless of how hurtful this might be to others.

Some variation in how individuals participate isn't usually a problem. The challenge comes when one or two members dominate the discussion and/or when one or two never participate at all. What should a facilitator do when faced with such situations? Needless to say, you are not going to change fundamental aspects of an individual's personality. Nor are you likely to create a meeting that somehow provides all individuals with the perfect balance of entry points, guidelines, freedom, and so on for their preferred forms of interaction.

As with the other challenges, the facilitator's goal is to create conditions— think of these as marking out a figurative "space"—that allow for balancing different types of participation.

POSSIBLE FACILITATION MOVES

Remind the group of relevant norms.

In Chapter 4, we discussed how setting norms can encourage all participants to feel supported in taking part in the meeting. In particular, norms such as "limit one's air time" or "make space in the discussion for all" can signal the importance of allowing for differences in the group. When participation feels particularly uneven, it can be helpful to invite the group to review the relevant norms and assess how it enacts them. (Chapter 4 and Chapter 6 have additional suggestions related to this move.)

Call for different modes of interaction during the meeting.

Even when the group generally observes norms like those cited above, some participants are less comfortable speaking in the group. The facilitator might suggest the group take some time during a meeting for individual writing and partner-talk ("pair-share"). Such moves allow even quiet participants to engage actively and also usually contribute to a richer discussion for every-one. Generally, in order to encourage depth, it is a good idea to limit pair-share discussion or writing to one or two questions related to the group's focus or topic.

Offer an explicit invitation to quieter group members to speak and/or make a specific request for more vocal group members to hold back.

The facilitator might also ask, before moving to a new activity or new step in a protocol, if anybody who has not spoken yet would like to say something. Conversely, parts of the meeting might be set up with an explicit request that no one speak twice until everyone has spoken at least once. (Note: There's a difference between encouraging people to speak and requiring them to. Even when the group does an activity like the "whip," in which each participant of-fers a question or comment one after another without discussion, it is usually a good idea to allow an option to "pass.")

Keep in mind that "quiet" does not necessarily indicate "unengaged."

Some people need more "think time" than others to formulate thoughts. Others feel they learn more by listening than by speaking. If the group has a participant who is persistently silent in the meeting, you might try touching base with her in between meetings. It might help her to understand that, al-though some silence is fine, the group needs, at least occasionally, to hear from her in the context of the meeting in order to be able to learn from and with her. You might explore what would make such (minimal) participation more comfortable for the participant—for instance, more group discussion in twos or threes or responding to a prompt in writing ahead of time.

By the same token, "vocal" doesn't necessarily indicate "uninterested in others' thoughts." A similar kind of conversation with participants who are ha-bitual talkers might help them understand the importance of monitoring their air time in order to leave some room for others to participate. The frequent speakers may have ideas for how you as facilitator can help them remember not to speak too often in the group.

Choose a good protocol.

Most protocols are designed with the goal of helping groups manage the ten-sions generated by these individual differences. A protocol such as the Tuning Protocol or the Ladder of Feedback (see Chapter 10) provides the opportunity to comment (at different points) from both a supportive stance and a more questioning stance. Such protocols can help participants practice engaging with one another in ways that convey respect and also encourage questioning and risk-taking. The Microlab Protocol can also help distribute speaking and listening opportunities more evenly among group members. (See *The Power of Protocols* and *Looking Together at Student Work* in Appendix: Resources.)

Some groups use an exercise to help participants become more conscious of how much they are (or are not) participating: They distribute a certain number of game chips or colored cards (perhaps two or three) to participants at the beginning of the meeting. Each time a group member speaks, she puts one of her chips or cards in the center of the table. When a participant has played all of her chips, she must remain quiet for the rest of the meeting. (Normally, this kind of activity is done as an occasional exercise rather than as an ongoing feature of meetings.)

Use a version of Listen-Describe-Invite-Propose.

This "facilitation routine" was introduced in Chapter 5. Drawing on the same set of steps, you might share with the group your sense that a balance is needed between making sure people are comfortable and empowering group members to challenge one another in healthy and respectful ways. Or you might describe your observation that some people are talking a lot while others are remaining quiet. Invite the group to share their perspectives on the situation and to suggest approaches or additional norms that might make it easier for everyone to engage in a more balanced conversation.

DIFFERENCES IN HOW INDIVIDUALS EXPERIENCE A GROUP'S AUTONOMY

Many teachers have had the experience of participating in voluntary groups. In some cases, these voluntary groups, such as study groups or teacher book groups, focus on key aspects of teaching and learning. Some teachers even choose to take part in such groups outside of their regular professional day. Teachers in these groups often describe them as providing some of their most powerful professional learning. This is true, at least in part, because the groups—and the individuals in them—have the autonomy to determine what the group will focus on (goals, questions, texts, and so on) and how it will do so (structure, process, roles). In other words, they feel ownership in the group's work.

Most teachers have also had the experience of participating in nonvoluntary groups—for example, grade-level teams, subject/discipline departments (typical in high schools), professional learning communities (PLCs), and other configurations. These groups are often marked by the same kinds of engagement as voluntary groups, especially when participants embrace the group's goals and processes and make them their own—in other words, when group members experience a sense of autonomy. (In Chapter 9, we consider some of the ways such groups can maintain or increase their autonomy in the face of outside demands.)

However, in other cases, teachers in such groups experience little or no autonomy to determine what the group will focus on and how, not to mention when the group will meet, where, or for how long. In part, this reflects the normal operations of a school: Each teacher is assigned to be part of at least one department, team, or group—it comes with the territory. But autonomy is also a function of the degree to which a group is able to determine how it will use its "mandatory" group time.

A group member's concern about a lack of autonomy can manifest itself in a number of ways that are unproductive—for example, an individual may withdraw from the group. This might take the form of a teacher physically isolating herself from the group, remaining silent within group meetings, or signaling that she is not engaging with the group—for example, checking email or grading papers during a meeting. It might also spur more active behaviors, such as questioning the value of the group's activity or the authority of the facilitator: "I'm here because I have to be." "This is pointless." "You can ask, but I don't have to answer."

There is no simple solution to either passive or more aggressive responses to a group's lack of autonomy (whether perceived or actual). Many of the possible facilitation moves identified in earlier sections, as well as in Chapter 5, may help address specific ways lack of autonomy may manifest itself—for example, withdrawing from the group or interacting in a dismissive manner. However, these may not help the group get to deeper questions about the degree of autonomy they have in their work. Below are two possible facilitation moves for helping a group understand and build its autonomy.

POSSIBLE FACILITATION MOVES

Bring it out in the open.

Issues of autonomy are likely to be less problematic if they are addressed openly. Consider devoting some or all of a meeting to a discussion of the expectations for the group's work: What are they? How have they been communicated? Who has a role in determining them? What are the implications for what the group focuses on? For the processes it uses? For what it produces?

Differentiate assumptions from realities, and act on realities.

In hierarchical settings like schools, it is often possible to act on the basis of assumptions about an administrator's or supervisor's expectations rather their actual expectations. It can be helpful to spend some time clarifying where expectations have been made explicit (for instance, in a memo or email or during a discussion with the facilitator or another group member). Depending on your read of the situation, you might also work with the group to develop a set of questions about the parameters for the group's work and bring them to a supervisor for discussion and clarification. On the other hand, some groups may choose to "fly below the radar" rather than bring it to the attention of an administrator that they are working away on their own goals. (This can be risky, and, if discovered, can initiate or contribute to tensions between the group participants and the administrator.)

On their own, these moves will not be enough to ensure the degree of autonomy that a group needs to pursue its own goals. We suggest you consider such moves starting places and that you continue to explore how questions of autonomy, or group interactions generally, relate to other contextual factors influencing the group. Chapter 9 and Chapter 10 offer more strategies for building autonomy in support of the group's learning, even in the most challenging situations.

Repurposing Meetings for Learning

The fundamental goal of facilitating for learning is always the same: helping a group take responsibility for, reflect on, and enhance its members' learning and the learning of their students. Some teacher group meetings are explicitly focused on this kind of learning—for example, study groups or collaborative inquiry groups. In these kinds of settings, the need for the kind of facilitation that supports the group's learning is obvious and crucial.

But not every teacher group has learning as its primary goal. Many groups are convened, often at the request of an administrator, in order to achieve a specific outcome—for example, a task force that is formed to identify the pros and cons of adopting a "one-to-one" (student-to-laptop) program in the school, or committee that is assigned to oversee the school's implementation of the new districtwide peer-mentoring initiative. And many standing meetings, such as grade-level team or department meetings, are similarly task-oriented, focusing on evaluating student data on standardized tests, developing common assessments, scheduling events for the upcoming semester, and so on.

Some of these purposes can feel removed from key questions about student and teacher learning. Fortunately, a group's stated purpose is not the only thing that determines how a group approaches its work. In Chapter 2, we discussed the importance of "stance"—the attitude or orientation toward the group's work that each individual member of the group and the group as a whole maintain. We identified two such stances: a *learning* stance and a *task-completion* stance. In the following sections, we consider how the facilitator can help groups to nurture the learning stance—to repurpose meetings to foster learning even when the group's stated goal is task-oriented. Facilitators do this not by abandoning the established tasks but by helping the group discover or create questions that are related to those tasks and that can be used to stimulate and guide the group's learning.

In this chapter, we address four common purposes for teacher groups (while recognizing that these are not the only ones for such groups):

- Analyzing student achievement data.
- Aligning curriculum and instruction with standards.

- Grading or scoring student work.
- Discussing individual students and their learning.

For each, we offer some possible facilitation moves that can help give teacher learning prominence in a group's process even as the group accomplishes the tasks associated with the identified purpose. Unlike earlier chapters, in which we describe relatively discrete possible moves a facilitator can take at a given moment, here we describe a range of broader moves (some of which might fill a whole meeting or several meetings) that a facilitator and group might use in response to particular situations.

ANALYZING STUDENT ACHIEVEMENT DATA

The growing emphasis on standardized testing of student achievement has resulted in more assessments for students to complete and, consequently, more data for schools and teachers to make sense of. Increasingly, teacher groups are asked to use the data from assessments to guide, or "drive," instruction. By examining the data, it is often argued, teachers will be able to adjust and target instruction to be more effective for all students.

A purpose ready-made for teacher learning, one might think. In reality, such meetings are often exercises in frustration. Teachers may be uncertain of how to analyze the data, critical of the assessments themselves, or even suspicious of administrators' motivations for the data analysis—is it the students who are being evaluated here or the teachers?

POSSIBLE FACILITATION MOVES

In situations that lack clarity about purpose and process, the facilitator might begin by suggesting that the group hold off on jumping into the work until everyone has formed a better idea of why the group is carrying out the data analysis. Three questions you, as facilitator, might ask to help establish a fruitful learning purpose and process are:

1. What questions might these data help us answer?
2. What process might help us address those questions?
3. What outcomes do we anticipate from the process, both in terms of our learning and our next steps?

For example, given data from a standardized writing assessment, a group might decide to answer the question, "What are the most significant obstacles for struggling learners?" To answer this question, the group might establish a process through which teachers identify "struggling learners" in their classes and then look for patterns in the data for those students. For example, do the students struggle with "main point," "support," "organization," or other dimensions of the task (which may be specified on a rubric)? Once major obstacles have been identified, next steps might include the following:

- Additional data gathering in order to understand why those particular obstacles are so difficult for students. (These data might include further samples of students' work, interviews or written reflections from students in which students describe their process, teachers' observations of students at work on related tasks, and so on.)
- A review of the strategies teachers currently use to support students' skill development in the dimensions of writing with which they most struggle and an analysis of which ones seem to be most effective for struggling students.
- A plan to investigate (through online research, face-to-face workshops, consultations with teachers in other departments, and so on) other strategies for supporting students in developing the writing skills with which they struggle most.

If no pattern emerges, this, too, can be a "finding." It may suggest that more data are needed to home in on the obstacles for these student writers. Again, writing samples from the group members' classes may provide the "data set" that helps the group address a question that the standardized assessment data did not. This is an outcome, even if it means more analysis. You might remind the group that data analysis usually raises more questions than it answers— and that being able to formulate new and better questions is as important an indicator of the group's learning as answering questions.

In another common scenario, a group might have a data set but may not be clear on how the data relate to the kinds of skills and knowledge they emphasize in their instruction. For example, in reviewing results on an 8th-grade math assessment, a group might find that students' algebraic skills are weak. The group might decide to explore the question, "How does what is being tested in terms of algebra relate to what and how we are teaching?" This might initiate a review of lesson plans, activities, materials, and so on.

ALIGNING CURRICULUM AND INSTRUCTION WITH STANDARDS

Planning curriculum can be a daunting task for teachers and groups, especially with the adoption by many states of the Common Core State Standards

(CCSS). Often, the stated or understood purpose for teacher meetings is "aligning" the curriculum with the standards. This can feel like a matching exercise, as teachers scour their lesson and unit plans for existing activities that at least plausibly relate to given standards—or might relate, with some tweaking or word-smithing. But how well does all this effort support teachers' learning about their curriculum content, their instruction, or their students' learning?

POSSIBLE FACILITATION MOVES

As in many situations, the facilitator's first task is to encourage the group to "put the brakes on"—that is, check a natural impulse to just get going with a task that might be seen, at least by some, as tedious, if not redundant. In order to repurpose the group's work as a learning activity, the facilitator might invite the group first to spend a few minutes reflecting on a question or two related to the purposes for the group's work—for example: What role should standards play in planning curriculum? What opportunities do standards offer us in our work to support student learning? What challenges do such standards pose in our work to support student learning?

The group's discussion of these questions will provide useful information for you and the group in determining the best process for your work. Borrowing the language of cinematography, we suggest two different strategies that might be generally useful:

- *"Zoom in."* In this process, one teacher volunteers to share a lesson plan (or activity plan), along with the standard(s) that she intends the lesson to address. The facilitator invites the group to identify and discuss how the cited standards are addressed in the lesson. Then she asks participants: (1) what questions they have about the lesson (in terms of how it addresses the standard), and (2) what questions they have about the standard (perhaps about definitions of terms used in the standard, the applicability of the standard to the particular subject area, and so on). This could easily be done with several teachers' lesson plans in succession within the same meeting.
- *"Pan out."* Rather than focus on one lesson plan at a time, the facilitator invites several teachers to volunteer to share copies of their lesson plans (or activity plans) that are designed to meet particular standards (the lesson plans do not all have to focus on the same standard). The facilitator invites the group to read through the whole batch of lesson plans with several questions in mind: What functions do the standards serve within the plans? Are there patterns in the ways that teachers have made use of the standards? What guidelines might

these examples suggest for how the group might use standards in the process of planning? (For similar "Slice" protocols, see *The Power of Protocols* in Appendix: Resources.)

In either of these strategies, it is important for the group to understand that the focus is not on evaluating the teacher's lesson or activity plan but rather on figuring out how to use the standards as a resource for the group's (and, ultimately, the students') learning.

In other cases, a group may be struggling with how to incorporate a targeted standard into a unit or lesson plan. Here are two processes a facilitator might propose to address this question:

- *"Back and forth."* The facilitator asks the group to identify a standard that at least two of the teachers in the group have or will include in a lesson or activity plan. Before looking at any plans, the facilitator asks the group to brainstorm the kinds of student performances that might address this standard. The facilitator should encourage teachers to be as specific as possible about what they would expect these student performances to look like. Then the facilitator invites the group to examine the plans and relate their expectations to the plans: How do the plans in their current form give students the opportunity to engage in the kinds of performances the group identified? In what other kinds of relevant performances do the plans engage students? How might the plans be revised to include more opportunities for student performances that address the targeted standard(s)?
- *"Working backward."* The facilitator asks a teacher to share a lesson plan (or activity plan) designed to meet specific standards but asks the teacher not to reveal those standards at first. As participants examine the plan, they discuss which standards seem most relevant to the content and tasks the teacher has shared. The presenting teacher listens to this part of the conversation for several minutes, before sharing the standards she had identified. If appropriate, the group might discuss how the plan could be modified to either relate more closely to the selected standard(s) and/or incorporate other standards in a meaningful way.

No matter the process used by the group, the outcomes should deepen teachers' understanding of the standards and the opportunities and challenges they present as resources for curriculum planning. Ideally, by using group processes like these, teachers end up not just with a set of lesson plans in which standards have been neatly inserted, but with models, tools, and questions that help them think through and plan curriculum, whether they are working individually or with colleagues.

GRADING OR SCORING STUDENT WORK

Teacher groups are frequently asked to grade or score students' work from across classrooms. There are a number of purposes for doing so, including calibrating grading ("getting on the same page") with a rubric or other scoring instrument, revising a rubric or developing a new one, identifying benchmark samples of student performance, scoring work from standardized assessments with reliability (i.e., "double scoring"), scoring work from a common assessment in order to analyze the results, and so on. Once again, it is easy for teacher groups to see such purposes as a chore, something to *get* through rather than *learn* through.

POSSIBLE FACILITATION MOVES

Having a conversation with the group about purpose is essential—especially when there are so many different purposes for working collaboratively to score or grade students' work. If the group has been asked by an administrator or someone else from outside the group to carry out this work, you might invite that person to the first meeting in order to understand her goal(s) more clearly.

Once the group is clear about the purpose, the facilitator might propose one of two general strategies to relate the purpose to the group's own (as yet unidentified) questions. The first general strategy takes as its starting place the mandated goals for the group. The facilitator might suggest the group use these given goals as a foundation for developing more specific questions about teaching and learning that group members would like to address. For example, you might ask: "Given that the principal would like us to calibrate our use of the new Common Core writing rubric, what are some questions about the rubric and its uses that we might want to explore as we work on calibration?" (Such questions might have to do with the definition of terms on the rubric, the relation of rubric dimensions to teachers' current student learning goals, and so forth.)

The second general strategy temporarily "brackets" the mandated purpose: Suggest that group members put it aside until they have brainstormed their questions that they might be able to explore through scoring work together. Then ask the group members to look for connections between their questions and the given purpose. The group might then consider ways that both the given purpose and the group's self-determined question(s) might be satisfied through its work.

Whichever path the group takes, it is important that you elicit questions that are meaningful for the teachers in the group and use these in proposing a process. These might be questions about using rubrics fairly and effectively, identifying students' strengths and weaknesses through assessment, definitions of terms, and others.

Here are two possible structures—both of which focus on scoring students' work, and either of which could be modified to also address the particular needs and questions that the group has identified for itself:

- *Scoring Conference Protocol.* A scoring conference is a useful process for developing a shared understanding of a rubric and how to use it. It supports groups in addressing questions about the rubric or scoring instrument—for example, how it relates to learning goals for students or targeted standards, how clear it is (to students and/or teachers using it), and how it can be used consistently and fairly. Using the Scoring Conference Protocol (Figure 9.1) involves selecting a few samples of students' work at different levels and making copies for the group. Then participants, working individually, score one student's work and discuss the scores afterward. They proceed to do the same with another student's work, and so on. The goal for the scoring conference is to allow individual scoring of students' work to generate discussion that responds to the group's question(s), not to achieve perfect reliability in using the instrument—although this protocol does help with this task as well. (It may be helpful for the facilitator to remind the group and any interested administrators about this fact.)
- *"Divide and conquer."* The facilitator distributes a set of students' work samples to teachers to score individually (choosing a reasonable number, given the time allotted, so that there is also time for discussion). As teachers report their individual scores, someone in the group records them on a table or chart. Depending on the group's purpose(s), the scores might be used as data to address any number of questions: Which students struggled? And with what? What are benchmarks for student performance? Which specific dimensions on the rubric were challenging to students? And so on.

Each of these approaches takes time. It might be wise to devote an entire meeting to the one the group chooses (and include time in the subsequent meeting for follow-up conversations). In either approach, a key task for the facilitator is to encourage participants to refrain from making assumptions about the students whose work is being scored or the reasons for the results that emerge from the process (for instance, "Students haven't learned how to . . . ," "This group of students tends to . . . ," and so forth). Keeping the conversation focused on exploring fully the samples of students' work and how that work is evaluated will enable a more thoughtful conversation at a later point about the conditions and circumstances that shaped the students' work (and how those conditions might be modified to allow for deeper student learning).

Figure 9.1. Scoring Conference Protocol

Purpose: To help a group establish a shared understanding of criteria for students' work and how students are assessed. In contrast to other protocols, this protocol is not geared toward giving the presenter specific feedback about her assignment; instead, the focus is on an assessment instrument (often, a rubric) and helping all teachers in the group calibrate their judgments about how to use the instrument in evaluating students' work. (Important: Make sure student names have been removed from work samples.)

1. Introduction

- Facilitator reviews the purpose for the protocol, the steps of the protocol, and the group norms.

2. Discussing the Assignment or Task

- Presenter briefly describes the assignment and its goals. (Presenter does not participate in the remainder of the discussion until the final reflection in Step 6.)
- Participants read the assignment/task.
- Participants discuss their expectations for high-quality responses to the assignment/task. (Group selects a note-taker to record the group's ideas.)

3. Discussing the Rubric/Instrument

- Participants examine the rubric (or other assessment instrument).
- Participants discuss how the rubric relates to the group's expectations for a high-quality response:
  - ✓ What did we discuss that does not appear on the rubric?
  - ✓ What appears on the rubric that we did not discuss?

4. Scoring and Discussing Student Work Sample—Round 1

- Each participant individually reviews Student Work Sample #1 and scores it using the rubric (or other assessment instrument).
- Participants take turns sharing scores for Sample #1 (recorder charts scores). The group discusses what evidence individuals used to arrive at their scores.
- Through discussion, the group strives for agreeing on a score for the paper.

5. Additional Rounds

- Repeat Step 4 with additional Student Work Samples (typically two to four samples total).

6. Reflections

- All participants (including the presenter) discuss what they have learned through scoring conference protocol:
  - ✓ What have we learned about our criteria?
  - ✓ What have we learned about our assessment instruments?
  - ✓ How has the protocol supported our learning?

Developed by David Allen and colleagues at the National Center for Restructuring Education, Schools, and Teaching (NCREST), Teachers College, Columbia University.

DISCUSSING INDIVIDUAL STUDENTS AND THEIR LEARNING

Teachers have always talked about their students with colleagues, whether describing an exceptional student performance, soliciting advice on how to reach a particular student, or sharing an anecdote about something funny (or disturbing) a student said or did in class. Typically, this kind of talk about students has been informal, often taking place in the hallways between classes or in the faculty room.

Increasingly, however, schools are making explicit the expectation that teachers talk about students as a strategy to support students' academic achievement. In grade-level teams and professional learning communities, time is devoted to discussing individual students who struggle academically and/or socially. Sometimes the group uses an explicit process (or protocol) for discussing students; sometimes not. Sometimes a counselor or administrator is included in the discussion; at others, only teachers. Much depends on the purpose for the discussion.

For example, in individualized educational program (IEP) conferences, the purpose is to develop an initial individualized plan or monitor how well the school is serving the student in relation to a plan that has already been developed. Because these meetings are often required in order to comply with state or district regulations, they usually follow a prescribed order and have a designated leader, typically an administrator or school counselor. Other discussions of students will be less formal—for example, discussions that take place as part of grade-level team. The group may agree to talk about a few students at each meeting, devote entire meetings to discussion of students, or talk about specific students as issues come up on an ad hoc basis.

POSSIBLE FACILITATION MOVES

Once again, the facilitator's first responsibility is to help the group become clear about the questions it hopes to address through conversation about students. You might remind the group that the most generative questions invite multiple perspectives and don't lend themselves to single definitive answers. Questions might address how a student has responded to specific instructional interventions or supports, what patterns emerge in a student's response to particular tasks or instructions, how a student interacts with classmates, and so on. The facilitator should remind the group that, in talking about a student, new questions will emerge and that these should be documented. Sometimes the questions that emerge in the course of a careful analysis of student work and behaviors turn out to be just as or even more important than the questions with which the conversation began.

Once the group is clear about the questions it hopes to address, you might propose a process that will help the group address them. One process intended to help a group discuss students systematically and thoughtfully is the team case conference. In a team case conference, the group typically follows these steps:

- A teacher presents a student about whom she has concerns, along with some evidence related to the student's performance and/or behavior (work samples, grades, observations of the student at work, and so on).
- Other teachers in the group who teach the student share their own observations about the student, again based on evidence.
- If appropriate and feasible, a counselor also shares information about the student that may help the group understand or contextualize the student's performance/behavior.
- The group develops a common understanding of the concern or problem.
- The group collectively develops specific strategies for how the teacher(s) will address the concern; these might be consolidated in a plan or timeline.

The group may also designate time in a future meeting to discuss how the strategies or plans are working. For a more detailed discussion of the team case conference, see *Supporting Students' Success Through Distributed Counseling* in Appendix: Resources.

Two other processes that can be used or adapted for examining and discussing students' work are:

- *Collaborative Assessment Conference.* The Collaborative Assessment Conference (Figure 9.2) has been used for a variety of purposes, including to explore the strengths and needs of a particular student and to foster conversations among faculty about what students are learning and how to support that learning. It provides a structure for a group to look together at a piece of student work, first to determine what it reveals about the student and what that student is working on, and then to consider the implications of that student's work for teaching and learning in general.
- *Descriptive Review Processes.* Descriptive Review Processes are useful but more challenging processes in which the facilitator (or "chair") not only guides the group through a specific series of steps for discussion of a student and/or her work but also extracts and summarizes key themes and questions for the group as it moves through the steps of the processes. (For more information, see *Prospect's Descriptive Processes*, included in Appendix: Resources.)

Figure 9.2. The Collaborative Assessment Conference

1. Getting started

- Facilitator reviews the purpose and steps of the protocol.
- Facilitator invites the presenter to share the work (though the presenter gives no context at this time).
- The participants observe or read the work in silence.

2. Describing the work

- Facilitator asks, "What do you see?"
- Participants offer observations without interpreting or evaluating the work.

3. Asking questions about the work

- Facilitator asks, "What questions does this work raise for you?"
- Participants state any questions they have about the work, the student, the assignment, and so on.
- Presenter does not answer the questions.

4. Speculating about what the student is working on

- Facilitator asks, "What do you think the student is working on? What is she most focused on?"
- Participants, drawing on their observation of the work, offer ideas.

5. Hearing from the presenter

- Presenter provides her perspective on the student's work and why she chose to share it.

6. Discussing implications for teaching and learning

- Facilitator invites all participants (including the presenter) to share any reflections/ questions the conversation has generated for them about their own work with students.

7. Reflecting on the Collaborative Assessment Conference

- Participants (including the presenter) reflect together on their experiences of or reactions to the protocol.

8. Thanking the presenter

- The session concludes with acknowledgment of and thanks to the presenter.

Developed by Steve Seidel and Harvard Project Zero colleagues

Whatever process the group uses, the facilitator plays a critical role in making sure the discussion heeds important principles:

- *Respect students.* The facilitator reminds the group that the discussion of students' work must be conducted in ways that accord students respect as human beings and maintain students' confidentiality. One way to encourage this attitude of respect is to develop a set of norms for talking about students (e.g., "Speak as though the student were in the room with us," "No name-calling, even in fun," and so on).

- *Use evidence, not assumptions.* The facilitator reminds the group to relate comments and questions about the student to evidence whenever possible (rather than making assumptions about students' motivations, past experiences, home lives, and so on). It is most effective to focus on "positive evidence"—that is, what has been observed or can be pointed to in the student's performance or work, rather than "negative evidence"—that is, what the student doesn't do (e.g., not handing in homework, not following directions, and so on).

- *Avoid the "blame game."* The facilitator also has a key role in making sure the discussion does not veer into ascribing blame (for example, blaming a teacher, the student, her parents, teachers in earlier grades, administrators, or others).

- *Move to action—but not too soon.* Usually in these discussions, the group moves naturally—and quickly—to problem solving. The facilitator helps make sure this shift does not occur too early, encouraging participants (often with the help of a protocol) not to jump to generating solutions before fully reviewing and discussing the evidence being shared. However, if the discussion does not generate next steps or new questions and ways to pursue them, then its purpose (and participants) will be frustrated. It is important for the group to understand that deciding that more evidence is necessary is, in fact, an action step—as long as the inquiry continues.

- *Reflect on learning.* Finally, the facilitator can encourage a learning discussion by suggesting that participants reflect on what they have learned through their discussion of the individual student. How might the group structure the discussion next time? What additional kind(s) of evidence would be helpful in discussing students? And so on.

By making her commitment to these principles explicit within the group and by modeling them throughout the conversation, the facilitator makes an important contribution to the learning stance of the group.

CHAPTER 10

Managing Challenges of School Context and Culture

In most of this book, we have explored the range of facilitation responsibilities involved in guiding meetings that focus on professional learning and the moves the facilitator makes in order to carry out those responsibilities. Although the facilitator's work is an important influence on the collegiality and productivity of meetings, at least as significant are the conditions within which the group carries out its work. These conditions can both support a group's work and pose challenges for it. In this chapter, we consider some of the common contextual challenges to a group's learning and how facilitators might help groups address them.

In the sections that follow, we examine challenges related to time, professional culture, and leadership. Each section includes one or more brief scenarios that illustrates the challenge. We consider some of the reasons each challenge emerges or persists. Then we discuss some of the ways facilitators might help the group address the challenge. Unlike in earlier chapters, where we describe possible facilitation moves—relatively discrete actions a facilitator can take at a given moment in a meeting—here, we focus on broader strategies that often involve discussions with stakeholders outside of the meeting, including administrators.

Of course, a definitive list of school-based challenges—and strategies to address them—would be beyond the scope of this book. So much depends on the combination of elements that makes each school unique—and uniquely challenging. And challenges of different categories will overlap and interact: For example, a school leader's lack of understanding of a group's work may lead directly to the infrequency of the group's meetings. Or a school culture of taking on many professional development initiatives may affect a leader's support for a teacher group that wants to pursue longer-term questions and goals.

One final word of caution: No one person can single-handedly change the cultural context of a given school or organization. The suggestions here offer strategies that can help manage some difficult situations, should you encounter them as a facilitator; however, for challenges like the ones described in this chapter, which extend well beyond the scope of a series of meetings, full resolution can come only through systemic and coordinated effort of the entire school community and its administrative and teacher leaders.

CHALLENGES RELATED TO TIME

Scenario: On Wednesday afternoons, your school alternates between whole-faculty meetings and department meetings. As the chair, you typically lead your department's hour-long meetings. At the beginning of the school year, your suggestion that the group pick a particular instructional issue on which to focus for the first semester was met with enthusiasm. Many colleagues seemed particularly interested in discussing critical reading skills and how to support weaker students in developing them.

Despite your best efforts and the group's enthusiasm, somehow the meeting time keeps slipping away. Last month, the principal pre-empted department meetings in favor of an additional whole-faculty meeting to discuss the district's new policy for addressing student absences. And then the department needed to give feedback on the textbooks being considered for adoption for next school year. Today, the group really needs to focus on getting the planning for the departmental midterm under way. Time is so scarce, and the urgent issues of the moment always seem to crowd out the important discussions of teaching and learning . . .

For schools that would like to implement teacher learning groups in a substantive way, finding the time for meetings that support teachers not only in getting things done but also in deepening their professional learning is the most-often-cited challenge. Meetings happen too infrequently, or are too short to accommodate all the different demands that need to be met.

There are actually two issues here: One has to do with how and when meetings take place. The other has to do with how the meeting time itself is spent.

Establishing a Time to Meet

When schools do manage to establish and sustain teacher learning groups, they usually deal with the time challenge in one of three ways: They "buy" time, "steal" time, or "make" time:

- *"Buy" time.* Schools that choose this approach usually manage to secure additional money to support teacher learning groups, either by obtaining grant funding or through careful and creative budgeting. The money is then used either: (1) to pay teachers for attending afterschool meetings, or (2) to hire a cadre of substitute teachers once or twice a month, who rotate through the building over the course of a day, freeing up groups of teachers to meet during the school day. Because of the additional resources that are involved, this is not a common approach, but some schools manage it.

- *"Steal" time.* In this approach, teachers simply meet either after school or on weekends, with no additional compensation for their time. Teachers who join such groups usually do so voluntarily, and sometimes such groups draw teachers together from across schools. Two of the best-known examples of this model are the Philadelphia Teachers Collective (Kanevsky, Strieb, & Wice, 2005) and Rounds at Project Zero (Seidel, 2010). Both groups have been running for more than 20 years. Though this approach is also uncommon, it offers a way for teachers who feel isolated in their schools to establish professional community and engage in ongoing learning with colleagues.
- *"Make" time.* This is by far the most common approach to dealing with the challenge of limited time. Groups carefully examine the meeting time that already exists within the school day—faculty meetings, department meetings, grade level meetings, and so forth—and ask: How could this time be used more effectively to achieve the group's most important goals? Almost always, groups engaged in this kind of reflective examination find that at least some valuable meeting time is spent on announcements, logistics, and other administrative details that could be handled via email or text message or some other communication method.

   To make time, groups often need to work with administrators, and perhaps even other groups, in considering how different meeting times are used for different purposes. If the school has two faculty meetings a month, one of those meetings might be designated for small learning group sessions. If a grade-level team has 45 minutes a week, they might agree to deal with their logistical and administrative issues in two meetings a month, reserving the other two for identifying and discussing important issues related to teaching and learning. In many places, a shortage of meeting time is less of an issue than is meeting time poorly spent.

Organize Time Within the Meeting

Given the difficulty of finding or creating new blocks of meeting time, how can a group do more with the time it does have? In Chapter 3, we suggest a number of facilitation moves for shaping a meeting agenda that helps the group focus on its most important goals. A brief recap of some of those moves:

- Before the meeting, invite the group's help in drafting an agenda and shaping meeting priorities and goals. A clear and common purpose can help the group stay focused.
- Use a good protocol. The Protocol Primer in Chapter 5 (Figure 5.1) provides a brief overview of protocols. Choosing an appropriate structure and making it explicit for the group can help minimize tangential discussions.
- Listen-Describe-Invite-Propose: This facilitation routine, introduced in Chapter 5, can be helpful in addressing the problem of competing priorities within a meeting when that problem is persistent. If you find yourself feeling like the group is always leaving important work undone or struggling for focus, describe your observations and feelings for the group and invite their thoughts: Are others feeling the same way? Do they have ideas about how to address the situation? The group's collaborative effort at problem solving might suggest some new strategies to try.

CHALLENGES RELATED TO SCHOOL CULTURE

Each school has its own unique professional culture—the norms, values, beliefs, traditions, and behaviors that influence how the adults in the school interact. Professional culture is shaped by many factors, including school leadership, the makeup of the faculty, partnerships with outside groups or organizations, the history of professional development initiatives, and many others. The culture, as much as organizational elements (how teacher groups are composed, how often they meet, and so on), creates the conditions within which professional learning takes place.

Scenario: Your 5th-grade team meetings are generally positive but hectic. In the space of 45 minutes, twice a week, the six teachers share information about upcoming school events or special projects in their classrooms, talk about students who need extra support (or are causing their teacher headaches), and bemoan the school and district administrators' decisions and policies. There is also a fair amount of talk about what's going on in teachers' lives outside of school and some generally good-natured ribbing. In the past, you have suggested the group use some more structured approaches, but the general consensus has been, "If it ain't broke, don't fix it."

Professional cultures in schools can range from truly collaborative to simply cordial to downright contentious. Most schools, like the one depicted above, tend to fall somewhere in the middle: Teachers and administrators get along with one another, communicate about schedules, discuss students (mostly informally), and perhaps share instructional resources, ideas, and strategies. However, except perhaps in pockets, these interactions often fall short of "joint work," as Judith Warren Little (1990) describes it: "encounters among teachers that rest on the shared responsibility for the work of teaching" (p. 519). In groups engaging in joint work, teachers regularly collaborate to solve problems, explore questions related to teaching and learning, and create new resources to support individual teachers and students in the school.

In situations like the one depicted in the scenario above, facilitators can help encourage a more collaborative mode with activities such as these:

- Share examples of practice and give one another feedback. The Ladder of Feedback (Figure 10.1) offers one structure for doing so. Another, more formal, structure is the Tuning Protocol (see *The Power of Protocols* and *Looking Together at Student Work* in Appendix: Resources).
- Talk about students in ways that support learning for the entire group. Chapter 9 provides some approaches and tools for talking about students positively and productively, including the Collaborative Assessment Conference and team case conferences.
- Engage in collective problem solving on a challenge that may affect more than one of the group participants. One tool that helps groups to do this is the Brainstorming Possibilities Protocol (see Figure 10.2).

Being clear about the group's goals will help you and the group choose the appropriate tool, keeping in mind that tools can be revised or reshaped to better address particular purposes.

Figure 10.1. The Ladder of Feedback

Purpose: To provide feedback about an idea, plan, or event
Time: Anywhere from 10 to 60 minutes

The idea or plan is presented to the group. Then the group moves through the following steps:

Step 1: Clarify: Ask clarifying questions to be sure you understand the idea or matter on the table.
Step 2: Value: Express what you like about the idea or matter at hand in specific terms. (Avoid offering perfunctory "Good, but . . ." and hurrying on to the negatives.)
Step 3: State concerns: State your puzzles and concerns. Use qualified terms: "I wonder if . . ." "It seems to me . . ." Stay focused on the specific aspects of what was presented.
Step 4: Suggest: Make suggestions about how to improve things.

Developed by David N. Perkins (adapted from *King Arthur's Round Table: How Collaborative Conversations Create Smart Organizations*, 2003)

Figure 10.2. Brainstorming Possibilities Protocol

Purpose: To share a puzzle, problem, or question and gather ideas from colleagues about possible action plans, solutions, or responses

Time: Varies. This version is timed for 15-minute "rounds" (enabling several people to share problems or questions and gather feedback in a single meeting). The protocol can also be longer or shorter.

1. Presenter *briefly* identifies the problem or question and provides a *little* context for the group. (Not more than 4 minutes. Shorter is better.)
2. Group asks a *few*, brief clarifying questions. (3 minutes)
3. The group brainstorms ideas, solutions, resources, and possible ways of responding to the issue. (6 minutes)

As they do so, the group observes the rules of brainstorming:

- State ideas briefly and succinctly. (No discussion.)
- No evaluating others' ideas—either to say they are good or bad or to agree or disagree.
- Work quickly. Keep the comments flowing fast and don't censor yourself. (No idea is too far-fetched to be shared in a brainstorm!)

Note: Presenter does not participate in the brainstorm but may want to take notes while ideas are being generated.

4. Presenter thanks the group for their thoughts (but does not give a response).
5. Brief debrief: Group members (including presenter and facilitator) reflect on how well they followed the brainstormed guidelines and what might improve the process in the next round. (1–2 minutes)

Once your group has tried one of these strategies, make sure to leave time for teachers to reflect on what worked, what didn't work, and what the group might change for the next time.

Scenario: Your 7th-/8th-grade PLC has been splitting its meeting time between looking at samples of students' work and "rounds," in which teachers observe one another's classes and offer feedback on a focus area determined by the teacher being observed. In addition, periodically all PLCs in the school have been analyzing data from the Common Core–aligned assessments in math and literacy to target instruction for struggling learners. The principal has recently returned from a leadership conference and is eager for your group also to pilot a "flipped curriculum," in which students review material online before class and use class time to apply that content in various activities.

What happens when a school takes on multiple new curricula, instructional programs, and/or professional development initiatives at the same time?

Groups charged with putting these curricula, strategies, or initiatives into practice lack time to adequately address the goals for all of them, and teachers feel stretched and stressed. You may be living in a "Christmas-tree professional culture," in which new initiatives are added like ornaments to a tree.

New strategies are always attractive—and may indeed be required to address student learning needs, especially if it seems existing ones are not gaining much traction. However, in professional cultures, it is typical to add new ones without taking any of the existing ones away, often because teachers are comfortable with these older strategies. "Less is more," Ted Sizer, founder of the Coalition of Essential Schools, wisely counseled teachers and administrators. He meant that students will learn more from going deeply into a smaller number of topics than by "covering" many. The same is true for teachers' professional learning.

Facilitators working within a Christmas-tree culture have several options to keep the group's meeting time focused on and conducive to learning. In milder cases, the suggestions for using meeting time productively identified in the section above may work. In more serious ones, a different approach is needed. Here are two that might be tried, an internal (keep-it-in-the-group) approach and an external (take-it-out-of-the-group) one:

- *Internal approach.* Use meeting time to investigate the goals for different initiatives, both ongoing and new. Try to crystallize the key goal or goals for each in terms of the professional learning they support (or might support). Map out a plan for meeting time that allows the group to address the goals. As a group, try to develop a sequence that will allow work on the different goals to coalesce—or at least not compete with one another. Document this plan (on chart paper or PowerPoint), so that the group can regularly revisit it and, as necessary, revise it.
- *External approach.* As a group, identify a reasonable number of initiatives to focus on. Develop a rationale for why these will make the most difference in teachers' instruction and students' learning. The facilitator, perhaps with other group members, can present the plan to the administrator and invite her questions and feedback.

Whatever approach, or combination of approaches, the group pursues, you have a responsibility, as facilitator, to remind those within the group (and perhaps those outside it) that the group's work is fundamentally about the professional learning of the teachers. This principle can easily be lost in the rush to try new strategies.

Scenario: You have been identified by your principal to facilitate weekly meetings of your high school's math department. When you ask about goals for the meetings, he says, "Just don't let them eat you up. Good luck." In your own experience, the meetings have been almost entirely spent complaining about the administration's ineptitude—the term *clueless* comes up often, and elicits a chuckle around the table. Other time is spent complaining about students' behavior. Some teachers don't even join the group, preferring to sit by themselves, grading their own students' work or reading a newspaper. Sometimes one of these teachers makes a quiet scoffing sound in response to a colleague's comment.

Fortunately, most teachers don't often experience situations like the one depicted above. But some do. The scenario describes a "toxic" professional culture, in which distrust and animosity between teachers and administrators, and often among teachers themselves, runs deep. In such cultures, teachers, feeling undervalued, often isolate themselves from one another or form factions.

Facilitating a group in such a culture is incredibly challenging, not least because the person charged with doing so may be identified as sympathetic to the administration. Any attempt to initiate discussions or activities may be viewed through a lens of suspicion and distrust.

In this extremely challenging situation, it may help to keep two things in mind: First, the resistance that might be directed toward you is not personal (no matter how personal it might feel to you). There are larger forces at work here, most of which are out of your control. If you avoid getting caught up emotionally in the tensions and grievances of the group, you might find that you are better able to use the Listen-Describe-Invite-Propose facilitation routine from Chapter 5 to help the group work through some of its challenges. Second, you as the facilitator are not responsible for "fixing" any particular complaints of group members. You are responsible for supporting the group's learning, not for solving individuals' problems—or the school's.

The facilitator must also recognize that, in such a situation, lack of trust is the fundamental issue. According to Bryk and Schneider (2003), "relational trust" in schools is built on four considerations: respect, personal regard, competence in core role responsibilities, and personal integrity. If the facilitator is to be trusted, she must model these attributes in her interactions with others in the group and within the school. Joining in the belittling of the administrators may create rapport with other teachers but will do little to build a foundation for relational trust.

A facilitator might begin by suggesting the group develop norms for how individuals will work together—for example, "Avoid 'trash-talking' about students, colleagues, or administrators." (See Chapter 4 for more on norms.) However, the idea of agreeing on norms may be rejected by some group members.

In such situations, the facilitator may be most effective by "thinking small," at least initially. You might identify a few teachers who will work with you on a short-term task that is likely to have immediate benefit to the teachers involved—for example, tweaking a problematic rubric, sharing some strategies that have been effective in getting students engaged, reviewing results of a recent assessment to identify areas in which students struggle, and so on.

These tasks should offer immediately applicable teaching ideas or resources. Once these activities are seen as useful, at least by a few teachers, it becomes more likely that others will begin to join the work in a positive manner. It is important to continually invite all teachers in the group to take part in these discussions, if only to diminish the chances that the active members are seen as an "in-group," and thus another source of distrust and acrimony.

In toxic cultures, students are the ultimate victims. The negativity that teachers and administrators feel toward one another can be projected onto the students, leading to dismissive or disparaging remarks about their behavior, their preparedness for school, even their intelligence. If nothing else, the facilitator working in a toxic culture can model a respect for the students as autonomous human beings, worthy of care and attention. If you do that, no matter what else happens, you will be contributing to the mitigation of a toxic professional culture. (*Coaching Whole School Change* in Appendix: Resources offers more strategies for making positive change in toxic cultures.)

CHALLENGES RELATED TO SCHOOL LEADERSHIP

Professional culture undoubtedly is strongly related to leadership, both affecting and affected by the ways leaders operate and communicate with teachers. As Linda Darling-Hammond (2014) writes, "Strong professional learning communities require leadership that establishes a vision, creates opportunities and expectations for joint work, and finds resources needed to support the work, including expertise and time to meet" (p. 13). In this section, we examine some challenges that arise when a school's leaders fail to establish such foundations for professional learning.

Scenario: The principal occasionally asks you, as facilitator of the 3rd-grade team, "How is it going with the Common Core training?" He adds, "It's going to be important that everybody is up to speed for the new assessments." When you try to explain that examining the Common Core standards is just one part of the group's work, and that the group doesn't actually use a "training" model, he brushes these comments aside. "Just let Alma [the assistant principal] know if there's anything you need."

Sometimes school leaders mistake a learning group's work for training, and the role of the facilitator of such a group for that of expert trainer. The facilitator has a few options in helping an administrator understand the purposes for the group's work, again offering a choice between internal approaches (inviting school leaders in) and external ones (bringing information about the group's work to the school leaders):

- *Internal approach*: Invite the administrator to a meeting of the group. Make sure that there are real activities on the agenda—the kind the group regularly engages in—as well as the opportunity for discussion with the group. The agenda should provide the visitor with a clear idea of the goals for the meeting as well as the learning activities that address these goals.
- *External approach*: Meet with the administrator (with another member of the group, if possible) outside of the group. Share artifacts from the group's work, including agendas, protocols, readings, and so forth. If possible, include some of the instructional resources the group has developed (tasks, assessment instruments, and so on) and/or findings from the group's inquiry or analysis of data.

The option of "flying below the radar"—that is, to quietly keep on doing what you're doing, no matter what the administration thinks is going on—may be tempting. However, if the disconnect between perception and reality is revealed, it can have negative consequences for the group (and for you as a facilitator), including imposed activities or a heightened level of supervision of the group's work.

Scenario: Your school's new principal is taking turns meeting with each of the school's PLCs. By the time she gets to your 8th-grade group, you've heard from other teachers that "there's a new sheriff in town," and she's demanding that groups devote their time to two activities: analyzing data from standardized assessments (interim and end-of-year) and planning activities that will boost student performance on the assessments in targeted areas. The principal tells the teachers, "All this 'soft stuff,' including looking at student work, talking about individual students, giving feedback on each other's instruction, is 'off the menu,' at least for the foreseeable future."

Lack of support for a group's learning often stems from a lack of understanding of it. Following the previous scenario, we identified some ways to help administrators develop that understanding. In the face of an unreflective or inflexible school leader, these strategies may not work. In a situation like the one above, in which the principal appears to demonstrate both these traits, another strategy may be called for. Here is one that may help:

- Take a step back, figuratively, and consider the possibility that the administrator is probably under pressure herself—for example, to bring up the school's test scores or demonstrate its alignment with district goals for curriculum and instruction.
- Look for ways to "repurpose" the group's work during meetings that will still address the demands for it made by the school leadership. Strategies for doing this in relation to specific purposes, which may be those your administrator has, are described in detail in Chapter 9. For example, the mandated purpose of analyzing student achievement data can often allow a group to address its own questions about student learning and instruction.
- Look out for "openings" for learning. These might take the form of questions a teacher asks or observations a teacher makes in the course of undertaking the mandated task. These might be fruitfully explored through a discussion during the group's meeting or become the basis for a discussion or activity during a future meeting. Simply asking the group at the end of the meeting for questions and observations, in writing and orally, may begin to build a reservoir for future learning activities.

Scenario: A colleague from your social studies department reveals that the principal has told another teacher in the group, "Don't worry too much about her (meaning you!). I'm going to be shaking things up soon."

There are many ways a school leader might demonstrate a lack of support for a facilitator, and many reasons for doing so: misunderstanding the facilitator's role and responsibilities, lack of confidence in the facilitator's competence, disagreement about priorities or approaches, resentment of the facilitator's esteem among colleagues, and others.

If you experience this as a facilitator, a first step is to request a meeting with the school leader. In this meeting, it will be essential for you to keep the discussion focused on the work, not on the personalities and personal histories involved. Easier said than done, to be sure, but try to "de-personalize" the situation: Talk about how your *practice* as a facilitator strives to support the group's professional learning (rather than, for example, how well liked you are by the group). Recognize that your efforts to do so won't be possible without the support of the school leaders.

If this fails, remember that you are not alone. Seek counsel from other teacher leaders. You may have recourse to a union representative as well. In your work with your group, keep your focus as much as possible on the learning and not the politics.

The challenges described in this chapter are large ones—most of which are rooted in long-established cultural or contextual forces that extend well beyond the reach of the individual facilitator of a teacher learning group. Even so, there are often ways to make small moves that shift the conversation or the group dynamic just enough to allow new questions to be asked and new insights to emerge. Contextual issues make the work of teacher learning groups difficult in many circumstances, but not wholly unfeasible.

Would it be better if all less-than-optimal school cultures could be completely transformed? Of course. But, as the saying goes, the perfect is the enemy of the possible. We argue that taking even small steps can create opportunities for teachers' professional learning.

CHAPTER 11

Voices of Experience

Throughout this book, we have shared our thinking about and practices for facilitating teacher learning groups. In doing so, we have been sharing what we have learned from many other facilitators whom we have had the privilege to observe and work with over the years. The lessons we have learned from these experiences have become so strongly integrated into our own practices that it is often difficult to say where one facilitator's move ends and another's begins.

In this final chapter, we draw more explicitly on the work of other facilitators. We asked some of the most experienced and skilled facilitators we know to respond to a few questions: What do you pay attention to while you are facilitating? What analogies or metaphors capture important aspects of how you think about facilitation? What gives you satisfaction or pleasure in facilitating teacher groups?

In the sections that follow, you will find some tips or strategies to apply in your own facilitation. More important, you will discover some of the ways expert facilitators think about facilitation. In a sense, we're convening a virtual discussion of facilitation, one we invite you to join.

ATTENTION

"There is a lot of setup stuff I pay attention to," offers Daniel Gray Wilson, director of Harvard Project Zero, who has facilitated a wide array of groups, from those composed of early childhood educators to those of university professors, as well as groups from business, the military, and professional sports. "I pay a lot of attention to what the goals and outcomes for the meeting are. Is this a decision-making conversation or a brainstorming conversation? Is it a straight-up sense-making conversation, where people are going to pool their perspectives and we're going to look for commonalities and differences?" Knowing the goals and outcomes helps Daniel "design interactions for specific purposes."

Terra Lynch was a teacher and facilitator of her colleagues at a New York City high school. Since then, she has worked with the Metropolitan Learning Center at New York University to help teachers and administrators develop facilitative leadership practices. Like Daniel Wilson, she focuses her attention on purpose:

> When people want to present a problem of practice, I always ask them to clarify if they are looking to better understand the problem, get next steps, or both. If both, I ask them how much of each do they want—50% understanding what the problem is and 50% next steps? 80/20? When the objectives of the presenter are clear to the group, the process goes more smoothly.

Gene Thompson-Grove, co-founder of the School Reform Initiative, has been facilitating teacher groups for 30 years. For Gene, attending to relationships is essential.

> One thing I pay attention to is people's affect. Are they smiling? Do they look pensive? And I wonder what that might mean. As people are leaving, I also notice if they are talking to each other about the content of the meeting and the work or learning they did together. There's something about this work that is fundamentally about relationship.

Miriam Raider-Roth, associate professor at the University of Cincinnati, has worked extensively with school-based groups, as well as with teacher study groups and seminars, and, more recently, video-based webinars. Miriam pays a great deal of attention to the group's "sense of community." The group needs "some way of becoming human to one another before we are learners. . . . I always start with some sort of check-in: How are you doing? . . . Just because in these spaces people are flying from one thing to the next."

Joan Soble served as a teacher for more than 30 years in Cambridge and other Boston-area public schools. During her last 10 years teaching, she also administered and supported the professional development program for Cambridge Rindge and Latin School (the public high school in Cambridge, Massachusetts). Like Miriam and Gene, she also attends to the group's relationships: "I'm paying attention to a certain level of affection in the group, which comes out sometimes as reassurance—group members reassuring one another—and sometimes as real honesty. In the groups that I thought went best, it felt to me like people in the group felt others *needed* them to think hard about issues—even if that thinking might make everyone a little uncomfortable."

Alan Dichter is a longtime New York City high school principal and more recently network leader for the City University of New York (CUNY) Network, which partners with the city's public schools. For Alan, "warm-up" activities, such as "Postcards" or "Connections," serve a dual purpose (see *The Power of Protocols*, for which Alan is a coauthor, in Appendix: Resources).

Yes, they help to build a sense of community within the group; at the same time, as facilitator, I'm doing a lot of research on the people in the group. That will help me make decisions later. . . . That's a piece of being a facilitator: constantly learning about the people in your group. It's like being a teacher: You're constantly learning about your kids while teaching. You are looking at the impact, and adjusting.

Beth Delforge has served as a classroom art teacher, a department chair, a principal, and a districtwide director of fine arts. Currently she is the Pk-12 Visual and Performing Arts program coordinator for Andover, Massachusetts, public schools. Like Alan, she focuses on the participants themselves: "As a facilitator, I'm trying to understand who the group members are. Facilitation involves an awful lot of assessment of the people you're working with: What are they interested in? What's their understanding of the topic being discussed? What are their needs? What's their comfort zone and tolerance for risk-taking?"

Debra Smith, a former teacher and teacher educator, currently head of the Program Evaluation and Research Group at Endicott College, also pays attention to individuals and how they are participating in the group: "I'm paying attention to whether there's space for everyone to contribute, not just those who are verbally quick. Hearing from those who take longer to process adds perspective that we don't always hear in conversations."

Joseph Schmidt is a veteran New York City high school social studies teacher and department chair, and now citywide instructional specialist for social studies in the New York City Department of Education's Office of Curriculum, Instruction, and Professional Learning. Joe pays particular attention to the questions that come up within a group's discussion: "It could be questions about process; it could be questions about whatever the content is of the meeting; or sometimes there are tangential questions that have real value because they may speak to larger themes or issues the group is working on."

Joan Soble described a similar focus on questions, balanced with the sharing of expertise:

I notice the degree to which everyone is wondering and also the degree to which people are acting as though they have some authority or expertise to share. The expertise doesn't have to be a huge thing—it might be a strategy that one teacher has that she can offer to another who is struggling with a particular problem. So I'm paying attention to how people are gauging when it's okay to wonder and question, and when it's okay to know something and not just to wonder about it.

For Gene Thompson-Grove, the silences are also important:

"I listen hard for silence . . . and what that silence might mean. Do people need more time? Do they not know what we're talking about? Are they thinking about the topic or question? My rule of thumb is to always give a few beats more than I'm comfortable with. When I'm about to interrupt the silence by saying something, I give it just a little more time."

There are many other things to pay attention to during the meeting. Joe Schmidt talks about the "nonverbal cues" participants might be giving: "the exasperated look, looking at your watch, checking your email, just not being truly present." Daniel Wilson pays particular attention to participants' "eye gaze": "Where is their focus of attention? . . . I'm scanning the room all the time: Where are people looking? Who are they looking at? And, typically, I'm trying to read attention and energy and make inferences about engagement."

Alan Dichter adds:

I also pay attention to my own listening. Nancy Mohr [Alan's wife, who died in 2003—a school principal and gifted facilitator] always told me: "Listen more, talk less." But *not* doing something is hard. What do you do instead? I learned an important, simple strategy from my good friend and cofacilitator Anthony Conelli: Take notes. Not only did it give me something to do when I wanted to talk, but it communicated a sense of respect and validation. More important, it actually helped me to recap at times. . . . I almost always found that what I had wanted to say during the discussion wasn't all that important after a few minutes, and when I did finally say something, it had a much better chance of being useful.

Like Alan Dichter, Beth Delforge pays attention to her own thoughts and reactions: "I listen to my curiosities and write them down. . . . I try to hold my preconceived notions at bay so I can trust the process and see what surfaces." She also pays particular attention to the group's challenges: "I notice how we handle the difficulties. Even when you're moving forward, it doesn't mean that you're not going to have hard conversations. Facilitation is a skill that can continue to develop over a lifetime. It takes conscious effort—sometimes everything works, sometimes it falls flat, even with experienced facilitators." Joan Soble concurs: "In a group that's working, I can make a mistake without losing my credibility as a facilitator. We can all just agree that we should have done something else instead, and then those observations contribute to the next session."

ANALOGIES AND METAPHORS

Facilitators often use analogies and metaphors in discussing the role or how they enact it. Perhaps this is because the job is notoriously difficult to define or explain. Not surprisingly, then, when we asked nine expert facilitators for an analogy or metaphor for their facilitation, we got more than twice that many!

Miriam Raider-Roth describes facilitation as "creating a space or helping the group to create the space. It is an invisible space, that sweet spot where you can feel that people are both being challenged and supported." One thing Miriam does to create that space is to help the group synthesize some of the "threads of the conversation. . . . If you see my hands during a meeting, it's like they are trying to pull things together. I don't have a word for that facilitation move but it's important."

Daniel Wilson also talked about facilitation in relation to designing space, much as an architect does:

> Architects, really good ones, spend a lot of time thinking about human beings, how they get fulfilled within spaces, and then design spaces to either amplify the desired human behaviors or allow opportunities for new behaviors to come forward. . . . Sometimes [as facilitators] we're designing physical spaces but more often we're designing mental spaces for people to inhabit, and it requires designing things that people can use in their interactions . . . .

Debra Smith draws on the design metaphor as well: "My orientation comes from my background in art and design. I think of a well-facilitated conversation in terms of form following function, or starting with the purpose and thinking about how the shape or design of the conversation can support that purpose. Designing a space, or a container for the conversation, that will hold people safely and keep them focused and moving forward."

Beth Delforge talks about a different kind of space: "As a facilitator, I hope our group becomes a kind of laboratory, where together, we can all explore new ideas, try out new questions, and see how things go. Not everything is going to work, but as long as we're learning and sharing results, it's a functioning lab."

Joe Schmidt introduces another analogy, relating facilitators to sandcastle artists:

> If someone asked me what is in a sandcastle artist's toolbox, besides a shovel, I would have no idea. However, I know she has an intricate and thought-out plan that has to allow for responding to situations and improvisation. I think facilitation is a bit like that: You have this very

interesting set of tools that may not look, on the surface, like they are tools at all. But in that particular moment when a tool is used, it makes perfect sense.

Joe continues to explore the sandcastle analogy: "I've never talked to one of those sandcastle artists but I believe their work is about process. Otherwise, why would they be working somewhere where eventually everything they make is going to disappear? Facilitation for learning is like that as well: It's about the process of learning; it's about helping the experience to thrive."

Terra Lynch offers another "making" analogy: Thanksgiving dinner. After describing the "prep work" that goes on before the group ("family and guests") convenes—especially figuring out what individuals are looking for from the experience and planning some opening activities—"then there's dinner!"

> Even if all the planning and prep has worked according to plan, you never know what moods and personalities will come into play. . . . I'm always ready to adjust and change as needed, depending on the group's vibe and individual responses to one another and to me. If I need to swap activities to bring the energy level up, I will. If I need to scrap a protocol, and create one on the fly, I will. And I will be transparent about it to the group, explaining why we are making changes. Or I will bring it to the group to decide. My goal is always to move toward more understanding, openness, transparency, and trust between myself and the individuals in the group, and to be clear about the purpose and outcomes of the day.

Like other facilitators' metaphors and analogies for the role, Alan Dichter's is a creative one:

> With facilitation, if it comes to the question of whether or not you reinvent the wheel, the answer is *yes*. As you think about each new meeting or new group discussion, yes, you have to invent or create the specific "wheel" or process or tool that will work for that group's purposes and context. But you don't have to reinvent the "round"—that is, the guiding principles (or paradoxes) of facilitation, for example, surfacing controversy while creating a safe environment for all participants.

Joan Soble continues the theme of creativity, but draws on a different medium—one that echoes Miriam Raider-Roth's hand gesture above: "I think of facilitation in terms of crocheting or weaving that leads to the creation of a fabric of interwoven fibers. The people in the group all contribute their different colors, and you can see both how those threads and colors connect and blend, and how they contrast and vary. The facilitator helps make sure all those yarns are linked together in some way, but it's a responsibility that is shared with the group members themselves."

Gene Thompson-Grove invokes another art form: "Sometimes the metaphor of dance is helpful . . . I'm paying attention to the rhythm, the dance, and the music. I'm not quite a conductor, because I don't exactly know where the conversation is going to go. But that idea of paying attention to rhythm is important."

Another kind of metaphor comes to mind when Gene reflects on the ever-increasing demands that are made on teachers' time and energy (many of which have little to do with supporting students' learning): "the oxygen mask on the plane . . . giving people time and space to breathe a little bit." In thinking about the quality of meetings, she asks, "Have we created an oasis of sorts where people feel respected and can do productive work at the same time?"

SATISFACTION

This book has naturally dwelt on some of the challenges of facilitation—and certainly there are many—along with occasional frustrations and moments of self-doubt. Why, then, are so many of the most talented and creative people we know drawn to facilitate groups of one kind or another? It is both appropriate and hopeful to conclude with some of the things that make facilitation satisfying, even enjoyable, for them.

Several facilitators talked about the satisfaction that comes when their role as facilitator seems less essential to the group's activity:

Alan Dichter: It's very satisfying when I do very little and learn a great deal.

Miriam Raider-Roth: Sometimes I know facilitation is working when I can stop facilitating.

Gene Thompson-Grove: As people are leaving the meeting, if the conversation is about them and the learning they have done—and not about me—then I know I have been successful.

Terra Lynch: Ultimately, I am a successful facilitator when I am no longer needed, because the teachers in the school are doing the work together, independent of me.

Joan Soble: It's satisfying when . . . people share responsibility for monitoring the group and how it lives by its norms and structures.

> It's always better when someone besides me says, "I felt in the discussion part of the protocol that we weren't really responding to each other, we were just taking turns talking."

Facilitators also take pleasure in a sense of "newness" that emerges within a group's activity. Miriam Raider-Roth says: "I feel such joy when teachers say, 'That was so helpful. I really feel like I'm in a new place' or 'we're in a new place as a group.'" Daniel Wilson puts it this way: "The emergent qualities of thinking are what I find really beautiful. When something new has come into the world that didn't previously exist . . . when a person is surprised by how they're thinking now and they're disclosing it to the group, or when there are five new ways that we're talking about something that previously we didn't know how to make sense of." Debra Smith concurs: "When people realize that they've gone somewhere new . . . there's a sense of magic in that discovery."

Beth Delforge shares similar thoughts: "I get pleasure in helping the group feel like the conversation . . . moved their thinking, surprised them intellectually. . . . When people are engrossed in someone else's work—demonstrating selflessness—it often . . . ends in new personal insights for everyone."

Joe Schmidt ties his satisfaction to the feedback he receives from the group: "Satisfaction comes from reading through feedback sheets after a meeting and seeing, not necessarily that I was successful, but that participants feel that their presence in that session, in that conversation, or in that moment, was useful to them and the group."

Though the individuals we interviewed are, without question, serious about their work as facilitators, they are also people who believe in the importance of fun in the work. Several called attention to the power or significance of laughter in a group's activity.

Terra Lynch told us that one of the things that indicates her facilitation is effective is when "participants are smiling and laughing, as well as quietly listening to a presenter or contemplating the particular topic or issue on which the group is focused."

Laughter, for Daniel Wilson, has "two important meanings in my role as facilitator. One is that it is celebratory and can connote a sense of togetherness and jubilation, which is really important in a group. Laughter can also serve as a nice mechanism to diffuse discomfort, which can also be important for a group's learning. So laughter can signal very different things but for a facilitator both are important."

Alan Dichter says: "I take a great pleasure in being able to use humor to tackle difficult and complex situations and to build community. People laughing with each other is an enormously powerful community builder, and if it happens in the context of the work, it humanizes the endeavor. And if we can laugh at ourselves, it's even better!"

Finally, the facilitators often referred to other facilitators they have worked with and learned from. These opportunities to observe, collaborate with, and talk to other facilitators are sources of great pleasure, as well as learning, for facilitators, the authors included. Our hope is that this brief chapter inspires more such conversations: within teachers' rooms, networks, workshops, institutes, online forums . . . wherever there is interest in helping groups learn.

Appendix: Resources

FACILITATION RESOURCES

Coaching Whole School Change: Lessons from a Small High School (2008). David Allen, Suzanne Wichterle Ort, Alexis Constantini, Jennie Reist, & Joseph Schmidt. New York, NY: Teachers College Press.

The Complete Facilitator's Handbook (1999). John Heron. London, UK: Kogan Page.

The Facilitator's Book of Questions: Tools for Looking Together at Student and Teacher Work (2004). David Allen & Tina Blythe. New York, NY: Teachers College Press.

Facilitator's Guide to Participatory Decision-making, Second edition (2007). Sam Kaner. San Francisco, CA: Jossey-Bass.

The Skilled Facilitator, New and Revised: A Comprehensive Resource for Consultants, Facilitators, Managers, and Coaches (2002). Roger Schwarz. San Francisco, CA: Jossey-Bass.

RESOURCES FOR TEACHER LEARNING GROUP MEETINGS

Print

Arts PROPEL: A Handbook for Music (1992). Harvard Project Zero. Cambridge, MA.

The Evidence Process: A Collaborative Approach to Understanding and Improving Teaching and Learning (2001). Harvard Project Zero. Cambridge, MA: Author.

Looking Together at Student Work, Third edition (2015). Tina Blythe, David Allen, & Barbara Schieffelin Powell. New York, NY: Teachers College Press.

King Arthur's Round Table: How Collaborative Conversations Create Smart Organizations (2003). David N. Perkins. Hoboken, NJ: Wiley.

Making Thinking Visible: How to Promote Engagement, Understanding, and Independence for All Learners (2011). Ron Ritchhart, Mark Church, & Karen Morrison. San Francisco, CA: Jossey-Bass.

The Power of Protocols: An Educator's Guide to Better Practice, Third edition (2013). Joseph P. McDonald, Nancy Mohr, Alan Dichter, & Elizabeth C. McDonald. New York, NY: Teachers College Press.

Prospect's Descriptive Processes: The Child, the Art of Teaching, and the Classroom and School, Revised edition (2011). Margaret Himley (Ed.). North Bennington, VT: The Prospect Center. Available at http://cdi.uvm.edu/resources/ProspectDescriptiveProcessesRevEd.pdf.

Protocols for Professional Learning (2009). Lois B. Easton. Alexandria, VA: Association for Supervision & Curriculum Development.

Resource and Protocol Book, Version 3.0 (2011). School Reform Initiative. Denver, CO.

Supporting Students' Success Through Distributed Counseling (2006). David Allen, Patrice Nichols, Charles Tocci, Dalia Hochman, & Kevin Gross. Lake Success, NY: Institute for Student Achievement.

Online

www.schoolreforminitiative.org. The School Reform Initiative maintains a website with a large number of discussion protocols for a range of purposes, along with resources for using the protocols.

References

Allen, D. (2016). The resourceful facilitator: Teacher leaders developing identities as facilitators of teacher peer groups. *Teachers and Teaching: Theory and Practice, 22*(1).

Ball, D. L., & Cohen, D. K. (1999). Developing practice, developing practitioners: Toward a practice-based theory of professional education. In G. Sykes & L. Darling-Hammond (Eds.), *Teaching as the learning profession: Handbook of policy and practice* (pp. 3–32). San Francisco, CA: Jossey-Bass.

Breidenstein, A., Fahey, K., Glickman, C., & Hensley, F. (2012). *Leading for powerful learning: A guide for instructional leaders.* New York, NY: Teachers College Press.

Brooks-Harris, J. E., & Stock-Ward, S. R. (1999). *Workshops: Designing and facilitating experiential learning.* Thousand Oaks, CA: Sage.

Bryk, A. S., & Schneider, B. (2003). Trust in schools: A core resource for school reform. *Educational Leadership, 60*(6), 40–45.

Cochran-Smith, M., & Lytle, S. L. (2009). *Inquiry as stance: Practitioner research in the next generation.* New York, NY: Teachers College Press.

Darling-Hammond, L. (2014). One piece of the whole: Teacher evaluation as part of a comprehensive system for teaching and learning. *American Education* (Spring), 4–13, 44. Available at https://edpolicy.stanford.edu/sites/default/files/publications/one-piece-whole.pdf

Dewey, J. (1934). *Art as experience.* New York, NY: Perigree.

Harvard Project Zero. (1992). *Arts PROPEL: A handbook for music.* Cambridge, MA: Author.

Heron, J. (1999). *The complete facilitator's handbook.* London, UK: Kogan Page.

John-Steiner, V. (2000). *Creative collaboration.* Oxford, England: Oxford University Press.

Kaner, S. (2007). *Facilitator's guide to participatory decision-making, 2nd ed.* San Francisco, CA: Jossey Bass.

Kanevsky, R., Strieb, L., & Wice, B. (2005). A Philadelphia story. In B. Engel & A. C. Marin (Eds.), *Holding values: What we mean by progressive education* (pp. 153–158). Portsmouth, NH: Heinemann.

Krechevsky, M., & Mardell, B. (2001). Four features of learning in groups. In C. Giudici, M. Krechevsky, & C. Rinaldi (Eds.), *Making learning visible: Children as individual and group learners* (pp. 278–283). Reggio Emilia, Italy: Reggio Children.

Little, J. W. (1990). The persistence of privacy: Autonomy and initiative in teachers' professional relations. *Teachers College Record, 91*(4), 509–536.

MacDonald, E. (2011). When nice won't suffice: Honest discourse is key to shifting school culture. *Journal of Staff Development, 32*(3), 45–51.

McDonald, J. P., Mohr, N. Dichter, A., & McDonald, E. C. (2013). *The power of protocols: An educator's guide to better practice, 3rd ed.* New York, NY: Teachers College Press.

Mehta, J. (2013). Why American education fails. *Foreign Affairs.* Available at http://www.foreignaffairs.com/articles/139113/jal-mehta/why-american-education-fails.

Perkins, D. N. (2003). *King Arthur's round table: How collaborative conversations create smart organizations.* San Francisco, CA: Wiley.

Ritchhart, R., Church, M., & Morrison, K. (2011). *Making thinking visible: How to promote engagement, understanding, and independence for all learners.* San Francisco, CA: Jossey-Bass.

School Reform Initiative. (2011). *Resource and protocol book, version 3.0.* Denver, CO.

Schwarz, R. (2002). *The skilled facilitator, new and revised: A comprehensive resource for consultants, facilitators, managers, and coaches.* San Francisco, CA: Jossey-Bass.

Seidel, S. (2010). Reflective inquiry in the round. In N. Lyons (Ed.), *Handbook of reflection and reflective inquiry: Mapping a way of knowing for professional reflective inquiry* (pp. 299–316). New York, NY: Springer.

Vanderkam, L. (December 12, 2012). 5 personalities that wreck a meeting. *CBS MoneyWatch.* Available at www.cbsnews.com/news/5-personalities-that-wreck-a-meeting/.

Villegas-Reimers, E. (2003). *Teacher professional development: An international review of the literature.* Paris, France: International Institute for Educational Planning, UNESCO.

Index

About the Authors

David Allen teaches at the College of Staten Island, City University of New York. His research focuses on collaborative teacher inquiry and facilitation of learning groups. He has been a researcher at the National Center for Restructuring Education, Schools and Teaching (NCREST), Teachers College, Columbia University; Project Zero, Harvard Graduate School of Education; and the Coalition of Essential Schools, Brown University. He has taught English language arts and English as a Second Language in middle school, secondary, college, and adult education settings. He received a Fulbright Fellowship to study school reform in Poland. His most recent books are *Looking Together at Student Work, Third Edition* (with Tina Blythe and Barbara S. Powell), *Powerful Teacher Learning: What the Theatre Arts Teach about Collaboration,* and *Coaching Whole School Change: Lessons from a Small High School.*

Tina Blythe is an adjunct lecturer at the Harvard Graduate School of Education. She develops and facilitates online professional development courses for Harvard Project Zero, where she spent 16 years as a researcher developing and studying approaches to nurturing deep understanding for both students and teachers. Her current work focuses on collaborative inquiry and facilitation. She consults for schools, districts, and organizations both nationally and internationally on issues of curriculum, assessment, and professional development for educators. She has taught middle and high school English and social studies in urban public and suburban independent schools. She has authored and coauthored a number of books, including *Looking Together at Student Work, Third Edition* (with David Allen and Barbara S. Powell), *The Facilitator's Book of Questions: Tools for Looking at Student and Teacher Work* (with David Allen), and *The Teaching for Understanding Guide* (translated into Spanish, Chinese, Swedish, and Georgian).